BIG LITTLE POLITICS

BIG LITTLE POLITICS

GOING LOCAL IN
A NATIONAL CLIMATE

ALEXANDER DEMIRCAN

NEW DEGREE PRESS

COPYRIGHT © 2019 ALEXANDER DEMIRCAN

BIG LITTLE POLITICS

Going Local in a National Climate

ISBN   978-1-64137-303-6   *Paperback*

          978-1-64137-585-6   *Ebook*

CONTENTS

HOW IT ALL STARTED   7

CHAPTER 1.   BRINGING THE LOCAL INTO THE NATIONAL   25

CHAPTER 2.   TURNING OFF THE TV AND "GOING TO
THE MOVIES"   43

CHAPTER 3.   CELEBRATING THE MOST WONDERFUL
TIME OF THE YEAR   63

CHAPTER 4.   SHEDDING LIGHT ON POLITICAL FIGURES   83

CHAPTER 5.   PUTTING COMMUNITY ABOVE POLITICS   101

CHAPTER 6.   THINKING OF IT AS AN EXTRACURRICULAR   117

CHAPTER 7.   FINDING MY COMMITTEE   135

CHAPTER 8.   RUNNING IN THE RIGHT DIRECTION   151

CHAPTER 9.   MAKING MEDIA THAT MATTERS   171

CHAPTER 10. GOING LOCAL   187

ACKNOWLEDGEMENTS   191

APPENDIX   195

INTRODUCTION:

HOW IT ALL STARTED

———

Most of my gym classes were spent floating around on the sidelines, trying to pass the period without getting caught for talking. The only sport I ever mastered was Wii Tennis. Hell, I even got cut from a team I only joined because "no one gets cut." All in all, I was never particularly athletic.

At the same time, I couldn't watch a game without die-hard rooting. If I detected my peers arguing over anything, I joined in, trying to pitch a case regardless of how limited my knowledge was. I'll even admit—I resorted to distraction, deception, and sabotage to win more games of "Capture the Flag" than I'm proud of. My aversion to sports was solely due to my own athletic incompetence. On the other hand, I could never pass up a hearty competition.

Growing up, I always wanted to play games. Video games, board games, strategy games, memory games, word games—you name it—all were in my wheelhouse. Competitors included my father (who never let me win), younger sister (who never won), friends, personal records, and countless Nintendo CPU players.

Then came 2008. Apple released its App Store, bringing a host of new gameplay straight to the comfort of my palm-sized iPod Touch. But when I wasn't playing Super Monkey Ball against strangers from all over the world, I started to notice a different sort of competition in the world around me. Unlike what I'd seen before, this one wasn't taking place on a football field, couldn't be ended by pressing the power button, and was certainly not produced by Hasbro.

President George W. Bush—elected when I was only 3 years old and whose name I only knew because it had been spray-painted on a few stop signs near my school—was about to leave office. What followed was a competition of epic proportions.

I saw candidates' debates, ads, and interviews; they made their cases and battled it out firsthand. I saw news coverage airing constantly in my home, where commentators spent hours splitting every last hair, from John Edwards' extra-marital affair to Hillary Clinton's wardrobe.

Most importantly, I saw the way my parents' dinner party conversations always seemed to devolve into verbal sparring matches. That's when I wanted in. So, I started bringing up the election on the middle school bus. By overhearing conversation hooks, I'd open discussions like, "Is McCain too old to handle being president?" or, "What has Obama done to prove he has enough experience?" At first, only a few bit the bait. By October, my morning bus sounded like a CNN panel, with a bunch of sixth graders battling it out across a literal aisle. While some only engaged because I provoked them, for me, this kind of behavior only increased into subsequent years. I joined Debate Club, and eventually was elected president. I realized I loved American History, particularly, learning about past presidents. For "U.S.A Day" during senior spirit week I designed a mock campaign sign, slapped a flag pin onto my suit, and went as a presidential candidate.I don't think I realized at the time how obsessed I was with presidents. The people who spent a lot of time around me probably did.

WHY IT ALL CHANGED

June 15th, 2015—the day of my high school graduation. June 16th, 2015—the day of the famed escalator ride in Trump Tower that prompted everyone in America to ask "Is he really serious?" Just as one chapter in my life closed, it seemed another was beginning.

Election season, here we come once again.Freshman year of college coincided with the leadup to the 2016 election, and boy was it memorable. Debates were viewed on common room TV's, primary results refreshed during lectures; I even remember my progressive friends hiding some Bernie merchandise around my dorm room while I was away for a weekend. I followed the developing race with my usual level of intensity but noticed that this time I wasn't the only one who cared. In fact, a lot of people seemed to care—perhaps even more than even I did. But still, I cared more than I ever had. For the first time, I could vote in a presidential election. This was a big deal for me since I no longer had to feel like I was living a lie by sporting my mother's "I Voted" sticker. While I continued to absorb FiveThirtyEight predictions and assume the role of fervent in-house residence hall pundit, the notion of evolving from spectator to participant excited me.

Now, most things about politics excited me. Watching campaign ads was exciting. Memorizing a list of all 100 U.S. Senators was exciting too. Voting, being the most fundamental level of participation, was understandably very exciting to me as well. However, I was also excited by the prospect of going one step further and actually getting involved.

In fact, it was during the 2016 election that I acted on my political hankerings and evolved into a proactive campaign volunteer. I was certainly not the only one who followed this path.On my campus and across the country, throngs of politically minded students flung themselves into campaign roles, elated to finally be old enough to participate in America's democratic process. With the entire nation's eyes on the battle for the presidency, it comes as no surprise that the bulk of college-aged aspirants directed their efforts here. For many passionate young people, the 2016 election represented their first foray into the political world. Wedded to a cause, willing to undertake even the most tedious jobs, and bearing a sense of vitality and enthusiasm, these fresh-faced political activists were vital to various presidential campaigns. As of August 30th, 2016, Hillary Clinton's campaign had 291 offices in fifteen battleground states; Donald Trump's had 88 (fewer, but still substantial).[1] These positions needed to be filled, and bright-eyed college labor forces were willing to do it.

My memories are this: passionate young activists mobilizing around Boston to drum up grassroots primary support for Bernie Sanders; busses departing from the Tufts campus with Hillary Clinton volunteers out to canvas quaint New Hampshire neighborhoods in advance of the general election. Finally, I recall despair enveloping masses of tired staffers as results came in, all absorbing the realization that their

---

1   Lisa Desjardins and Daniel Bush. 2016. "The Trump Campaign Has A Ground-Game Problem". PBS Newshour. Accessed October 11 2019. https://www.pbs.org/newshour/politics/trump-campaign-has-ground-game-problem.

time and efforts had failed, with little to leave with beyond titles like "Field Organizer" or "Campaign Fellow" on their resumes. Here's the twist: this wasn't me. Though I witnessed these events unfold firsthand, the stories above are not mine. Instead, my time and effort was committed to a political cause that the presidential junkie inside of me never would have imagined.

HOW I ENDED UP WHERE I DID

In the lead-up to 2016, I was absolutely on track to become one of the people mentioned above. My competitive spirit—and gross athletic incompetence—had me deploying words and ideas as battle weapons. In past elections, I'd even temporarily turned my Instagram into a campaign coverage account. My already extreme television watching habits skyrocketed as countless hours were spent watching the news. To me, presidential politics was the American political system's apex, commanding more prestige and importance than anything under it.

As the summer of 2016 approached, my fellow college freshmen began selecting internships. Amid peers in computer science, economics, and pre-med, I firmly fit within the political box. My path seemed to be a no-brainer: I spent hours filtering through summer campaign opportunities online. In the end, landing a role wouldn't be as easy as I thought.

I am from Connecticut—one of the least relevant places in the world of presidential elections. Solidly blue since 1992, it is the absolute opposite of a contested battleground. For this presidential campaign, the best opportunities were in swing states—places like Ohio and Nevada—that seemed a bit far for someone who thought going to college two hours from home was a bit of a stretch.

My research was also an education in the duties given to campaign volunteers. In these grand scale campaigns, decision-makers are far from those on-the-ground. As a staffer or volunteer, you're only one of many phone-bankers, door-knockers, or email-senders. It's a pretty big deal to even see your candidate in person, let alone meet them. Careers are ladders that need to be climbed, but this was a few rungs below where even I wanted to start. Most importantly, by summertime, primary campaigns were winding down, and we knew who our nominees would be. Presidential elections are always about side-picking—don't get me wrong, that's a huge part of why they're so fun—but 2016 put division on full display. With "Lock Her Up" chanted on one side, and a "basket of deplorables" shamed by the other, Americans truly turned against each other on the public stage.

Unfortunately, neither side appealed enough for me to commit my labor to them. Traveling to a swing state, working amongst hundreds of other volunteers, completing menial tasks for little to no compensation, and engaging in political polarization—all are justifiable when you steadfastly support the cause. When you don't, it just doesn't seem worth it.

Despite these setbacks, I wasn't ready to abandon my political plan just yet. My parents were longtime friends with a man named Tom Dudchik—a longtime political insider and founder of "CT Capitol Report," a state news website and television program. As a fixture in Connecticut's political scene, he had heard about my political hankerings and suggested I orient my vision locally, even though I had no prior connection to the politics of my community.While the majority of Americans were wholly consumed with the top-of-the-ticket presidential race, we in Connecticut had a senator up for re-election, along with all five congresspeople. Moreover, *every* seat in the State Legislature—36 seats in the State Senate, 151 in the General Assembly—were on the line. All of these elections were happening the same day we voted for our next president, but I, like most others, gave them fractional attention.That is, until Tom Dudchik introduced me to Chris Healy, who was overseeing all Republican State Senate campaigns in Connecticut. Chris Healy then introduced me to candidate Lorraine Marchetti, who was running in my home district. I recognized her name from Town Council and Board of Education rosters over the years but knew nothing about her, besides that she was an active citizen within the community. I was so removed from town that I didn't even know she was running for anything.

Though they weren't political figures in my own community, Dudchik and Healy put me on the right track, pointing me right back to where I came from: Glastonbury, Connecticut. The school year ended, and after the major ordeal of leaving home just a few months earlier, I was already moving back. I didn't know what exactly I would spend my summer doing—except that rather than working for Clinton or Trump, I was working for Marchetti.Though I spent that summer doing something I had never considered before, and it ended up being my most rewarding experience, and the first domino of a long chain that ultimately led to the conception of this book.

HOW I SPENT THE SUMMER

Though Connecticut isn't a "swing state," it still has "swing districts," that make for exciting and competitive races. Since 1960, Republicans have had a majority in the State Senate only three times, for a total of six years spanning half a century. 2016 was a watershed year because if Republicans could flip four „swing districts" from blue to red, the majority would be theirs.This knowledge was enough to kick my competitive instincts into overdrive. Matters like these don't receive widespread attention, but that doesn't mean they don't exist. We're all familiar with the tensions in scoring the 270 electoral votes necessary to win the U.S. House and Senate. The same forces are at play on a smaller scale, grounded in every state of the nation, outside the sight of national news medias.

Lorraine Marchetti challenged a three-term Democrat incumbent, closely aligned with the state's deeply unpopular governor. Under that governor's leadership, I had witnessed a state in decline for the past six years. It was a place my out-of-state friends repeatedly mocked, and in-state friends dreamt of escaping. It was the butt of too many "high taxes" and "bad infrastructure" jokes that started out funny but eventually just made me sad.

This election seemed to have the potential to change that, and to me, this cause was worthy enough to fight for. Those summer months were essentially a crash course in local politics. This was largely thanks to the experienced, knowledgeable, and helpful candidate and her team, but also in part due to smaller scale of a local campaign. In all campaigns, from presidential to municipal, there's money to raise, a budget to maintain, a platform to build, and messaging to spread. The biggest difference is, there are fewer voters to reach and fewer people to reach them.On a presidential campaign, I probably would've been one of a few thousand "coordinators", repeating the same jobs over and over, to reach more people. Here, I didn't have a title, and tackled whatever was thrown my way. While I still made phone calls and went door-to-door, I also spent most of my time one-on-one with the candidate. I completed administrative tasks, but also ventured out and attended public events. I even had a seat at campaign team meetings, where there was the chance to give direct input and even spearhead projects of my own. It was a huge privilege to be given so many responsibilities, in so many different areas. I found, though, that if you're willing to work, there's *always* something more that can be done on a campaign.

The most valuable experience, to me, was traveling around the four-town district with Lorraine as she made public appearances and connected with voters. Whether it was a Farmer's Market in the rural community of Andover or the annual "Peach Festival" in the small city of Manchester, I stood beside Lorraine, carrying her belongings, snapping pictures and videos of her interactions, and passing out palm cards. This gave me the chance to observe local politicians in communication with constituents. This connection doesn't happen from a stage or while surrounded by TV cameras—it happens face-to-face, informally, and accessibly. Throughout, I felt incredibly empowered: getting to watch local politics from up close for the first time. The presidential election was still on my radar (old habits are hard to break), but it did lose some of its luster. The federal race appeared less important and less natural, compared to what I lived and breathed on a daily basis.

HOW AN ELECTION CHANGED EVERYTHING

The true moment everything changed was when I returned home from college for Election Day weekend in November. I had drastically reduced my role on Lorraine Marchetti's campaign after summer ended; I now knew I needed to return for the final stretch. The days preceding Election Day buzzed with frantic excitement. I remember visiting campaign headquarters (which had moved from the Marchetti's home office to an empty bank while I was gone), delivering lawn signs, and doing some last-minute door in neighborhoods that had gone untouched. On the big day I rose bright and early—proudly donned my "Lorraine Marchetti for State Senate" t-shirt—and stood with the team outside my former middle school, waving at residents as they went in to vote.

After a treacherous drive from Party City, with two-dozen red and blue balloons violently bobbing around in my backseat, I arrived at the results party. While friends, supporters, and party members flooded the golf-course clubhouse, I sat with a few others, all clenching our cell phones, in an anxiety-ridden corner. As the night went on, calls and texts rolled in, reporting the results. These statistics were then entered into a spreadsheet and projected onto a screen, for the whole room to see. I'd always seen results-reporting as the most official and confidential element of campaigning, so to see them pop up in real-time on my phone had me geeking out.

The candidates were neck and neck, but even after all precincts had reported results, we still had to wait for one final count: absentee ballots. I was sent immediately to Glastonbury Town Hall, where ballots were being hand-counted, so we could obtain the results as quickly as possible. After absentee counts from the incumbent's hometown were reported, he was placed a few hundred votes in the lead. Everything was riding on the count I was sent to retrieve. As I walked through the dark, empty corridors of my town hall at almost midnight on Election Day, I thought about how it felt every other time I was there. This time, I wasn't there to submit a passport application or accompany my mother to submit our property taxes. This time, I was there as an adult, to collect election results. This time, a candidate was waiting on me to find out if she won or lost. Now, I'm a pretty impatient person. It should come as no surprise that waiting over an hour for huge news, in an empty hallway, after an exhausting day was no easy feat. As I sat there, reflecting, I came to a realization: It was midnight on Election Day, and I had not thought *at all* about the presidential race. In fact, I had barely thought about it all weekend. Instead, I was thinking about how I—an 18-year-old college student—was going to be the first person to know the results of this election. I also could not stop thinking about how I had the responsibility of breaking it to everyone else.

I arrived back at the viewing party at around one in the morning, to a somber scene. Though loss is never easy, a narrow loss is particularly difficult to stomach. When Lorraine Marchetti garnered 49.38 percent of the vote, it was the definition of narrow.[2] Since three other "swing districts" flipped—we ended up only a few hundred votes away from reclaiming the majority. As I shared a melancholic hug with Lorraine, she thanked me for all my help, and I thanked her in return. I didn't want this campaign to be over, and I was already craving more.

That's when I knew this life is for me.It was at this point that I truly came to realize the power of local politics. I had the chance to work personally with a candidate who was running for a position most people don't care much about, despite its pretty significant impact. In doing so, I sharpened my professional skills, connected more fundamentally with a community I never appreciated enough, fought for a cause I truly believed in, and took a step away from the unprecedented levels of counterproductive polarization sweeping America.All of this ultimately taught me about another way to take political action, one dismissed by some and never even considered by others.

---

2 "Connecticut State Senate District 4 – Ballotpedia". 2019. Ballotpedia. Accessed October 11 2019. https://ballotpedia.org/Connecticut_State_Senate_District_4.

From that point forward, I knew my progression into the political world would start locally. To me, local elections represent American politics in their truest, purest, most grounded form.

After the 2016 election, I withdrew from national politics for a while, mainly because I enjoyed local politics a hell of a lot more. While everyone was focused on what was happening up-top, I had my sights set below, on municipal issues, races for State Representative or State Senate, and local party chapters.

Over the next few years my involvement in municipal and state politics only grew: meeting more people, working on more campaigns, and learning more lessons about this country and its government than I thought possible. Each year I saw something different, and, just three years after first setting foot on a campaign, I ended up managing one myself, in none other than Glastonbury.

WHY LOCAL IS BETTER

In writing this book, I'm aware not everyone started off the way I did (obsessed with presidential elections). However, by highlighting the local path into politics I hope to offer a new perspective to people at every level of political involvement.

Maybe you come from my prior position—consumed by national politics but dismissive of local, deeming it less interesting and lower stakes. My goal for those readers is to demonstrate that if you like national politics, you'll most likely enjoy local politics too. It possesses all of the same elements, but on a more manageable scale. The candidates, the issues, and the campaigns are all within reach, rather than hundreds of miles away.Maybe you dislike politics entirely, or at least think you do. You're probably drawn to the negatives: the corruption, attacks, hypocrisy, scandals, and division it can breed. You might find it stressful and frustrating; politics might even prompt a desire within you to move to Canada. I want these readers to realize that although there are a lot of reasons to feel this way, it's a misconception to think of *all* politicking as negative. Many officials, candidates, and volunteers are good people who volunteer their time to local causes. Local politics can be a source of building friendships, meeting people, and understanding where you come from.Finally, you may be reading this as someone already involved, and a lot of this information won't be new. If you're one of those readers, I hope to accurately highlight the positive work that you do. Within this book is the much-needed recognition of a special group of Americans who—more often than not—don't receive as much attention as they deserve.

HOW THIS WILL WORK

In subsequent chapters, I share more about my journey, stories, and takeaways from progressing along this path. I also highlight some of the figures who I got to know along the way, sharing their words and lessons. Finally, I profile others—both in my area and beyond—who exemplify this book's message. You'll find that rather than include as many stories as possible, I focus on a few in greater depth. This is because, with such a wide-reaching subject, it's impossible to convey information about every relevant figure in every corner of America. In going in-depth on myself and a few others, I hope to instill a comprehensive sense of the important impact of local politics. Then, wherever you are, hopefully you can recognize, encounter, and hear from the people around you too.

If this book is a journey, the first leg will be spent cultivating an awareness of local politics—something we all should have but in reality few actually do. In focusing on local issues, local elections, and local political figures, misconceptions can be cleared and confusions can be demystified. As spectators, we can all take simple steps to bring us closer to the individuals and issues shaping the world around us. In doing so, we ultimately become more informed and grounded citizens.

The second leg is designed to take things one step further. Once awareness is built, it becomes easier to consider translating thought into action. By highlighting the accessibility and diversity of opportunities, I hope to shed light on the great things that happen behind the scenes and anyone who's interested can get in on. There are always ways to help yourself, your community, and your country by stepping into the local scene. If I learned anything in 2016 it's that—in politics—sometimes things that seem little can actually make the biggest impact.

CHAPTER 1:

BRINGING THE LOCAL INTO THE NATIONAL

———

When the Founding Fathers set out to design the American government, their focus was largely local. Rather than centralizing power *a la* Britain, governance was instead given to localities who could better represent the interests of their people.

Since then, a lot has changed. Over generations our eyes have become increasingly fixated on national politics. We now drink mainstream media coverage like it's water, invest ourselves in distant causes unlikely to affect our lives, and overestimate the importance of the president. This dynamic has caused some to grow obsessed, others to grow apathetic. I'll go on to explain why and how this happened, but more importantly whether this trend can be reversed. Local politics, local issues, and local officials deserve more attention than they receive. In a time when Americans from across the spectrum have little faith in politics, giving the local our time, attention, and effort is the way forward.

It starts with recognizing the important function local politics serves. Because of the smaller scale on which the local operates, this can be difficult. Fortunately, one moment we all experienced together can put this into perspective. This moment may have happened when everyone was focusing on the national, but also sheds much-needed light onto the local.

WHY WE CAN THANK A PRESIDENTIAL CANDIDATE

One afternoon, I was skimming over David Hume's *Treatise on Human Nature* while focusing more on what was playing through my headphones (nothing unusual there). "They call me Mayor Pete," I listened "I'm a proud son of South Bend, Indiana, and I am running for president of the United States."[3] On April 14th, 2019, I watched this moment unfold via Facebook Live, along with thousands across America.

---

3   Tom McCarthy and Martin Pengelly. 2019. "'They Call Me Mayor Pete': Buttigieg Launches 2020 Presidential Run". The Guardian. Accessed October 11 2019. https://www.theguardian.com/us-news/2019/apr/14/pete-buttigieg-2020-presidential-campaign-launch.

A mere three months earlier, few knew Pete Buttigieg. In fact, I would've been incredibly doubtful of hearing 'mayor,' 'South Bend, Indiana,' and 'president' in the same sentence.

For the most part, this is a book about local politics. It makes the case that—despite being widely discounted and neglected—the local is a fascinating, accessible, and fruitful place to direct your attention and efforts. It is, however, important to note that no discussion of politics is complete without acknowledging the non-local: trends, issues, and moments broadcasted on national news—consumed by Floridians and Alaskans alike. Nothing exemplifies this better than the presidential campaign trail. Just as we can count on the sun to rise each morning, presidential hopefuls will announce their candidacies every four years. This usually happens right after midterms, as the public is quick to pivot its attention from one major election to the next. As citizens, we all respond differently to this parade of announcements. Some of us feel rather neutrally towards the subject: only reading headlines and notifications to stay topically aware of who's hat is in the ring. Others are completely unconcerned, accepting that the field inevitably narrows, and deeming it a waste of time to be educated on candidates who will only last a few months. Then there are people like me, who find few moments *more* exciting than these announcements. This interest, for me, stems from a combination of my desire to remain fully engaged and my pure love for the sport of it all.

In a way, the process is similar to watching players step up to a poker table in Las Vegas. There are always the high rollers, entering with loads of chips and intimidation; then there are the has-been's, sticking around but not quite serious contenders. Finally, there are the underdogs and a few surprise players thrown into the mix. Anyone is free to spectate—all you need to do is turn on breaking news notifications, constantly refresh Facebook, and invest time in reading reports and expert analysis. This inevitably ends up annoying those around you who care less, but I think that's a price worth paying.

WHY THIS CANDIDACY IS DIFFERENT

As I watched Buttigieg formally announce his candidacy—despite having an essay on Hume due the next day—I thought back to what had happened since Buttigieg launched his exploratory committee in January, when he first stepped into this national spotlight. In poker terms, he entered the race as both an underdog *and* a surprise player. That said, he soon proved stand-out in a crowd packed with senators, governors, and congresspeople. Some lauded his measured articulation; others appreciated the history he made as the first openly gay presidential candidate.

Witnessing this has made me happy—not because I'm a steadfast Buttigieg supporter, but because of *what* his candidacy has signified.

After carefully watching the 2008, 2012, and 2016 elections as well as studying the preceding ones, I've grown fluent in the trends and patterns that underlie presidential candidacies. Many believe the most fundamental shaking of orthodox presidential politics happened when Donald Trump was elected. However, while his victory was unprecedented, his candidacy was not. Successful business moguls who have never held elected office, running as "outsider" candidates have been around long before Trump. Such figures include Ross Perot in 1992, Herman Cain in 2008, and Carly Fiorina who herself ran against Trump in 2016. Buttigieg's candidacy, however, is different from what we've seen in past elections. He too is an outsider, but one unlike President Trump was. In fact, Buttigieg has been quick to assert he has "more experience in government that the president of the United States, [...] more years of executive experience than the vice president and [...] more military experience than anybody who's arrived behind that desk since George H.W. Bush."[4] Neither is he an outsider akin to Bernie Sanders—Buttigieg's views and positions do not veer too far from the mainstream, making him ideologically "on the fringe."

Instead, his status as outsider is a simply a matter of scale.

---

4   "2020 Hopeful Pete Buttigieg Touts "More Experience In Government" Than Trump". 2019. Cbsnews.Com. Accessed October 11 2019. https://www.cbsnews.com/news/indiana-mayor-pete-buttigieg-touts-more-experience-in-government-than-trump/.

We've seen mayors run for president before: Rudy Giuliani in 2008 and Bill de Blasio in 2020. Both led New York—a city with over eight million residents, outnumbering the respective individual populations of all but twelve states. In contrast, Pete Buttigieg's town—South Bend in Indiana—has a population of just over 100,000. He is, by and large, a local politician, no different from the politicians I chat with at community events or see walking out of a town council meeting. We all live in municipalities governed by officials like this, but many of us often just don't think of them.Buttigieg's candidacy has called attention to this class of local leaders, to those working in local governments, across all American localities. The overwhelming majority of them won't run for president—at least not without ranking higher first—but the fact that *this* one has, and is being taken seriously, is remarkable.

This has, in turn, led to my exceptional curiosity for the why's and how's of Pete Buttigieg's candidacy.

HOW HE GOT HERE

When Pete Buttigieg launched his presidential exploratory committee in January 2019, we had no idea who he was, let alone how to pronounce his name. That was until a string of televised town halls, a firestorm of video interviews, and an aggressive push to normalize his difficult, Maltese surname (it's BOOT-EDGE-EDGE, at least that's what's printed on all his merchandise). The thirty-seven-year-old mayor of South Bend, Indiana, formally announced his candidacy in April and suddenly became a serious contender in an unprecedentedly crowded field. As I dove into his biography—tracing his trajectory—I grew increasingly impressed by the Indiana mayor's noteworthy splash into national spotlight.

In many ways, Buttigieg's candidacy reinforces the notion that local political involvement is nothing to sneer at. His story illustrates the personal, communal, and national merit of engaging in hometown arenas.

Hovering only two years above the qualifying age limit for presidential candidates and only having held municipal office, Buttigieg's résumé is undoubtedly jarring upon first glance. Recall, for example, the uproar surrounding Barack Obama's "inexperience" as a first term senator seeking the nomination in 2008. However, though Buttigieg is just a local official in a small, Midwestern city, he has nevertheless garnered substantial experience over his few years in politics. When summoning the image of a politician, you'd most likely imagine someone in their fifties, sixties, or seventies. Buttigieg obviously does not fit this mold. He was first elected mayor in 2011— age twenty-nine—becoming the youngest mayor of a U.S. city with a population over 100,000. This wasn't merely a municipal board position or seat on a council; Buttigieg was elected to run an entire city at an age when most haven't even run a household.

The son of Notre Dame Professors, Buttigieg grew up in post-industrial, working class South Bend. During his childhood, he, "did not really realize that abandoned factories or empty houses were unusual," since, "that was just part of the furniture."[5] Despite his local roots, Buttigieg's life was by no means static. Upon graduating high school, he went on to study history and literature at Harvard. After graduating this time, he went on to study as a Rhodes Scholar at Oxford. Then, he took a high-profile consulting job with the renowned firm McKinsey and Company.

Over this coming-of-age period, Buttigieg maintained an interest in politics and worked on a number of campaigns. In 2010, after three years at the firm and a decade after going off to college and the world beyond, he moved back to South Bend in pursuit of elected office.

5   "Presidential Hopeful Pete Buttigieg Talks 2020, New Memoir | Season 2019 Episode 02/13/2019 | Chicago Tonight". 2019. PBS.Org. Accessed October 11 2019. https://www.pbs.org/video/presidential-hopeful-pete-buttigieg-talks-2020-new-memoir-ky/.

Many unique shifts Buttigieg made at this time seem to defy logic. One was his career jump from a notoriously high-paying field, to a categorically low-paying one. Another was the geographic shift from East Coast to Rust Belt. Such decisions, however, make sense when you appreciate and admire politics at its core.

Buttigieg's cites his interest in public service as a product of his admiration of President John F. Kennedy. In calling upon his Catholic upbringing and tenure at Harvard's Institute of Politics, Buttigieg has drawn historical inspiration from the Kennedian notion that, "a whole generation then was motivated to run by the idea that public service was noble."[6]

Today, a dangerously pervasive perception exists that politics is dirty. This has, in turn, perpetuated a self-fulfilling prophecy in which politics has attracted more cynical, power-hungry individuals, in it for the wrong reasons. This dynamic is more present in Washington, D.C. than in the fifty states, which tend to be governed by people on the ground. As a politically motivated young professional, Buttigieg could easily have moved to D.C. as a lobbyist or congressperson's chief of staff. Instead, he went back to

---

6   "Pete Buttigieg, "Shortest Way Home"". 2019. Youtube. Accessed October 11 2019. https://www.youtube.com/watch?v=Nldx3r7h3Cg.

Indiana. Buttigieg's first foray into campaigning was in 2010, running for Indiana State Treasurer. Compelled to stand up for autoworkers neglected by the incumbent, the twenty-eight-year-old Buttigieg decided to seek public office. As a Democrat challenging a sitting Republican in a state-wide race, in red-as-tomato Indiana, Buttigieg's bid was unsuccessful. That said, many politicians acknowledge that loss is not discouraging; it's actually motivating. Buttigieg recognized this failure as crucial experience, and says he, "learned about the value of standing up for what you believe in even when you can't make it." He sees this treasurer's race as the time when he, as a first-time office seeker, had a chance to "cut his teeth." Buttigieg was well poised to try again in the following year, on a more localized level.[7] He did, and this time was successful.When he ran for far-from-glamorous mayor of South Bend, Buttigieg faced the profound challenge of seeking to lead a place News-week deemed one of "America's Dying Cities." Buttigieg reflected that, "To me, that was a rallying cry, and instead of trying to wish it away, I talked about it every day I was campaigning."[8] Treating the city's status as a wake-up call that demanded fresh, new leadership to resolve, the articulate and determined Buttigieg soared to popularity among disillusioned constituents who'd watched their hometown

7   "Presidential Hopeful Pete Buttigieg Talks 2020, New Memoir | Season 2019 Episode 02/13/2019 | Chicago Tonight".
8   Ibid.

slowly crumble for decades. Committed to reaching voters at an individual level, Buttigieg portrayed himself as an unjaded newcomer, armed with academic credentials, an appetite for progress, and a knack for leadership. He contributed a new perspective to a city and government entrenched in the past.

HOW IT WENT

In his two terms in office, Buttigieg effectively modernized a dying, Rust Belt city into a mini-metropolis by spurring private development. He not only improved the city's infrastructural health, but also prioritized the needs and concerns of his constituents, asserting that, "As a Midwestern mayor from a millennial generation, I view politics not as theoretical but personal."[9]

Buttigieg's personal success was largely cultivated by his transition from private to public sector. As an Ivy League graduate working at a premiere consulting firm, the world was truly his oyster. However, the notion of noble public service instead guided Buttigieg towards a different kind of success. Rather than advancing as a cog in the corporate machine,

---

9   Pete Buttigieg. 2017. "Hitting Home: A New Politics Of The Everyday". Medium. Accessed October 11 2019. https://medium.com/the-moment-by-pete-for-america/ hitting-home-a-new-politics-of-the-everyday-76316121f06a.

he became a local leader. While a business executive may find fulfillment in paychecks, a local leader experiences fulfillment elsewhere: from directly serving their constituents.

When a six-year-old boy was rushed into South Bend Memorial Hospital in critical condition, doctors were unable to communicate with his Arabic-speaking parents. An interpreter was desperately needed, and doctors sent messages out on the emergency scanner system to find one. Fortunately, their calls were expediently answered by someone who overheard the commotion—multilingual mayor, Pete Buttigieg.

Emergency room physician Dr. Donald Zimmer remembers how Buttigieg, "translated words that I said, and words that the patient's mother said, without imposing himself into the dialogue at all. What he did that day was not at all about him."[10] Though not within the mayor's job description, this act not only serves as a testament to Buttigieg's character, but also as an illustration of the close relationship that can arise between constituents and local leadership. It's important for we— as citizens—to understand our political structure is larger than what's shown on CSPAN and that Capitol Hill's cushioned bubble is not a complete representation of all politicians.

---

10 "How Does South Bend Feel About 'Mayor Pete' For President?". 2019. Youtube. Accessed October 11 2019. https://www.youtube.com/watch?v=cgMuPErHxZY&t=81s.

Though Buttigieg's proximity to his constituents makes unique stories such as the one prior possible, he is also responsible for problems exclusive to municipal executives. The greatest obstacle he has faced on the presidential campaign trail involves the killing of a black man by a white South Bend police officer. Facing passionate criticism from his constituents and other Americans, Buttigieg has responded to heated demands like, "Reorganize your [police] department by Friday of next week," and, "Get the people that are racists off the streets."[11] While a senator's biggest challenge during a run for president is answering for their voting record, a mayor is responsible for visible, tangible problems affecting people in the most direct way possible. Regardless of where you stand on policing, this scandal exemplifies a crucial fact: local politics is not easy. While challenges faced by the president are apparent in the media every single day, local officials must instead be more directly connected to their constituents.

Like with the above medical case, this relationship can sometimes produce heartwarming results. In other similar situations, the results can be gut-wrenching. Buttigieg's rise to national stage, as will be discussed, calls attention to

---

11 Nathalie Baptiste. 2019. "Why South Bend's Police Department Has Become A Campaign Issue For Mayor Pete". Mother Jones. Accessed October 11 2019. https://www.motherjones.com/politics/2019/07/why-south-bends-police-department-has-become-a-campaign-issue-for-mayor-pete/.

both the positives and negatives that consume local politics. This paradigm extends far beyond a single mayoral record; Buttigieg's mayoral challenges are also dealt with by local officials across the country. This type of recognition can hopefully raise awareness on local politics matters that are all-too-often glazed over. Thousands of people have been refreshed to see Buttigieg step onto the field, contributing a local perspective to national conversation. He appeared as such a stark departure from the norm, they were surprised such a politician even existed.

But they do, and you don't need to travel very far to find them.

If Pete Buttigieg hadn't run for president—thus opening his mayoral record to national scrutiny—many Americans would be almost entirely oblivious to local politics.

WHY LOCAL IS SPECIAL

For better or worse, politics is more personal on a local level than anywhere else. Sometimes, it's visible when an elected official steps up from their desk to venture into communities to directly engage with constituents. This personal touch is also crucially important on the campaign trail. It isn't only a voter's job to pay more attention— improvements must also be made by officials and candidates themselves. Unfortunately, some local candidates underestimate the gravity of their positions and run unknown to the majority of voters. Though many make an active effort to rally attention even when the odds are stacked against them, the inactivity, complacency, and neglect of some perpetuates political apathy among voters, who tend neither to know nor care about local representation.

This can only be remedied by learning from Buttigieg's example and approaching politics with enthusiasm, care, personal connection. While Pete Buttigieg did just that in a quiet corner of Indiana, this type of thing can and should be done everywhere. In pivoting his efforts towards the presidency, Buttigieg's local experience distinguished his outlook and rhetoric among a pack comprised mostly of Washington insiders. While representatives often spend their days engaged in futile Congressional battles, so much of local politics rides on the need to devise tangible and pragmatic solutions to close-to-home problems spanning from sidewalk construction to public school budgeting to sewage maintenance.

As a massive nation of closely-knit communities, America depends on local officials serving them. Unfortunately, these officials are low priority to most Americans, who tend to be captivated by the more dramatic and attention-grabbing federal politics.

But even though these figures capture most of our political attention, Buttigieg acknowledged that, "in communities like [his]... national politicians were talking too little about us and too much about each other, and themselves."[12] This encapsulates why there is so much value in going local.

HOW TO LEARN FROM THIS

In examining Pete Buttigieg's political ascent, I profiled but one government official. This official embarked on a journey into the world of local politics and found personal fulfillment and professional success. While his journey culminated in a run for president, there are thousands of stories out there of inspired individuals stepping up in their respective towns and cities, but without recognition. Beyond politicians, this inspiring class includes campaign staffers, party officials, and mobilized volunteers. Though their views may differ, these people share the goal of involving themselves with the lowest tiers of government, all to serve their communities. That was *not* the conclusion I expected to reach while researching yet another presidential candidate. Especially when most take the same path up the political ladder. This difference only reinforces just how remarkable local political leaders can be.

---

12   Buttigieg, *"Hitting Home: A New Politics Of The Everyday"*.

Unlike many, I know who my local representatives are. I've read about them, I've met them, I've even campaigned for some of them. On the other hand, I know a lot of disengaged locals who nevertheless also obsessively consume presidential election coverage. While there is absolutely nothing wrong with that, let Pete Buttigieg's plunge into the national pool serve as a reminder not to ignore the local scene— it may affect your future to an enormous degree.

WHY I CARE SO MUCH

Though I only have experience as a campaign volunteer in Connecticut, this book tells the stories of figures from all the aforementioned categories, both within my home state and in other corners of the nation. While local issues and governmental structures will vary by location, I am concerned with highlighting commonalities transcending geographic boundaries: paths taken by average citizens into political spheres, trials and tribulations of campaign trails, and impacts of civic involvement on both those who serve and those served. Today, political literacy is crucial and political involvement is accessible. Rapidly changing cultural tides and technological innovation have significantly altered the political process by welcoming all demographics into the political world and modernizing involvement. However, to take advantage of the modern landscape, we must first distance ourselves from partisan hostility. This hostility has absolutely pervaded the national discussion and taken us farther away from the grounded, participatory political structure as created by the Founding Fathers.

Pete Buttigieg has demonstrated great things are possible with the power of local politics. From translating civic awareness to civic appreciation to civic action, even an Indiana mayor can have a solid shot at becoming presidential nominee. Buttigieg may be the current "golden boy" of local politics, but he doesn't have to be the only one. In localizing our attention and efforts, we can all come to understand the importance of our nearest layer of politics, and even go on to directly engage with it.

CHAPTER 2:

TURNING OFF THE TV AND "GOING TO THE MOVIES"

——

If one thing is clear, it's that there are not many things that we can all agree on. As fiercely opinionated people with a penchant for exercising free speech, Americans love to debate just about anything—even an issue as trivial as how to eat an Oreo. While the art of disagreement is deeply ingrained in our nation's fabric, and particularly foundational to our interactive political systems, I may have discovered one truth that Americans might agree with:

Politics is unavoidable.

We are met with constant reminders of this statement. Every time a television is turned on, a newspaper is opened, or a social media feed is refreshed, a Pandora's Box of news, commentary, and propaganda is unleashed, whether we avidly consume it or not—we are met with it. Though it may seem counterintuitive, as someone who *does* like it (and purposely seeks it out), I think this is a great problem to have. Even though keeping up with Washington D.C. is important, and political fans among us should absolutely not turn a just blind eye to the issues of national importance, there is great value in paying more attention to nearby politics.

WHY THERE'S A PROBLEM WITH THE STATUS QUO

This problem stems from the kinds of matters that receive such widespread attention. Major political news that captures media and citizen attention alike is almost always on the national scale. Furthermore, this news is typically highly controversial in nature, sure to inflame passions and spark fierce disagreements on both televised panels and at dining room tables across the country. Whether the day's big story centers on a high-profile candidate, a White House scandal, a Congressional squabble, or a foreign policy dilemma, word of it is guaranteed to permeate all channels of communication. This phenomenon is relatively straightforward. National issues are the only matters that affect all

Americans, so of course major news sources will devote their resources to reporting on them. Of those hallmark issues, those entrenched in controversy and polarization monopolize attention for their intrigue and complexity. They lead to more viewership, which leads to more money.

Consider the look and sound of cable news pundit panels. First, a "hot topic" is introduced by a smooth-talking host, whether it's a candidate's debate performance, a president's statement, or a recent tragic event. Then, commentators from various positions across the political spectrum give their takes, raising voices and surface-level clashing, but unable to explore the topic deeply due to time constraints. Finally, the host closes the segment, typically giving the last word to the panelist whose leanings are most in agreement with theirs or their network's. Turn on CNN, MSNBC, or Fox News right after you read this and see for yourself.

This paradigm has become an unshakable pillar of the mainstream news cycle. The problem is not the existence of heated pundit panels. In fact, I find great fun in watching them; I commend contributors with whom I agree and roll my eyes at those I don't. However, their omnipresence is detrimental for these reasons: they're entertaining, they reinforce existing beliefs, and they pit opposing views against one another. These are all things that news—in its rawest form—should not do.

Commentating is not reporting; commentators are *not* held to the ethical standards of journalists who must provide "only the facts" and are instead encouraged to interject with opinions no matter how baseless or outlandish.[13]

Unfortunately, when many seek political awareness, this is where they turn. It's accessible—airing on multiple channels, every hour of the day. It's also engaging—a 5-minute long MSNBC panel is far more viewer-friendly than a 5-hour long C-SPAN congressional hearing. In turn, media like this (opinion-laden and dramatized), monopolizes our political attention spans. Some of us get overly invested and become stubborn, militant followers. Others are appalled by the mud-slinging and negativity, closing themselves off from anything remotely political.This represents just one way things have spiraled over the years, when it comes to political engagement. With major issues dramatized, exaggerated, and sometimes even fabricated, American political integrity has significantly dwindled. Those in power are partially to blame—gridlock, obstructionism, and corrupt politics have inflamed tensions among Americans and tainted our democracy. However, this problem has been tremendously exacerbated and perpetuated by media outlets, who have

13   Graydon, Shari. 2010. "Commentary Vs Reporting". Informedopinions.Org. Accessed October 11 2019. https://informedopinions.org/commentary-vs-reporting/.

exploited serious political problems for the sake of entertainment and increased viewership.

As the byproduct of America's interactive political structure, two-party system, and freedom of press, this is nothing too new. But things have gotten worse. In order to understand how we got here, it's important to look to the past.

HOW WE GOT HERE

For over a century after America's birth, print news dominated as the exclusive means of spreading political information; it remained reasonably objective (though used extensively for campaigning purposes and featuring occasional cartoons). By the early 1900's, however, newspapers began deploying sensationalist and muckraking techniques to pique consumer interest. Beginning in the 1920's, radio revolutionized political news. It allowed Americans to directly hear from reporters, and—beginning with FDR's Fireside Chats—elected officials themselves. In the mid-century, television provided an even newer frontier for political news conveyance, though was initially limited to a few major stations. Tides began to turn in the 1990's and 2000's, which saw the advent of polarizing cable television news stations (such as Fox News and MSNBC), opinion-driven online journalism, and politically inflammatory radio shows. Through marketing outrage to specific ideological sects rather than diverse, general audiences, the entire civilian discourse surrounding politics changed. Everyone did not have to rely on broadcast news stations who attempted to appeal to the country as a whole.

The days of every family on the block tuning into CBS Evening News with Walter Cronkite after supper are long gone. Since things sounded a lot more interesting when the stories shown and opinions provided emphasized a certain ideology, the media took a turn in that direction. This only intensified past 2010, as social media provided a public platform accessible for all civilians to use. Not only did volume and accessibility of political news transform, so did the process of how it's created by opening the floor up to impassioned, homegrown journalists. Today, my newsfeed is flooded with political posts, articles, and memes—each possessing lengthy comment chains, brimming with incendiary words from all ideologies. With the glut of stories available and unprecedented ease in posting them online, the troubling phenomenon of "fake news" has gained traction.People like seeing things they agree with. Over time, this has become easier and easier for political consumers to do. The wide array of sources allow for the self-segregation of media consumers—different population segments receive different sets of information about matters that should be universally presented.

Nowadays, it's even difficult to take news reports seriously. I find myself constantly assuming every story is spun, with facts distorted and details omitted in order to serve political aims. The consequence is somewhat of a lose-lose situation: consume too little and you won't know the whole story, or consume too much to avoid these biases and sacrifice all of your free time.

WHY THIS IS BAD FOR OUR POLITICAL HEALTH

As this brief history indicates, politics is becoming harder to avoid, something that only makes our population angrier. Some fall victim to fearmongering tactics, completely and overzealously buying into the outrage. Though technically politically engaged, it's far too easy to fall down the rabbit hole by devouring flashy headlines and provocative video snippets, only to parrot misleading information in the form of rambling Facebook posts and unproductive arguments. This dynamic only strengthens ideological divisions, not to mention unnecessarily raising stress-levels. For many years, I was one of these people. I simply thought *this* was what politics was all about: picking an ideology and fighting for it, cheering at Fox News and booing MSNBC, and asking peers pointed political questions to see allegiances. Unsurprisingly, this made me one of the more unpopular kids on the school bus.

Alternately, others grow disillusioned and disenchanted—becoming political nihilists. I saw this happen with my mother. As my father would fall asleep watching Fox News, the squawking and fighting would sometimes wake her up and cause an anxious sickness. During the day, she would go places like her book club, where literary discussion would take a backseat to brutal and demonizing political battles. Over time, her political tolerance was chipped away. Even if aware of the importance of remaining engaged, some are simply unable to remain in the crossfire. Many roll their eyes at breaking news alerts, switch channels when a campaign ad comes on, and even drive right their place on Election Day. They've been around long enough to know that every tragedy is followed by a politicized explanation, every victory followed by one party diminishing the other's success. Though these people are able to resist biting the political bait, simply ignoring and opting-out of civic engagement is certainly not the answer either.

In a 2014 report on political polarization, Pew Research found that, "those at both the left and right ends of the spectrum, who together comprise about 20% of the public overall, have a greater impact on the political process than do those with more mixed ideological views."[14] This means that, for the most part, politics across all levels is being

---

14 Amy Mitchell, Jeffery Gottfried, Jocelyn Kiley, and Katerina Eva Matsa. 2014. "Political Polarization & Media Habits". Pew Research

driven by the most hyper-polarized among us. They are the most likely to vote, most likely to donate to campaigns, and most likely to physically participate, either as a volunteer or as an official.[15]

Though a glance at TV, Facebook, or fellow book club members may make it seem Americans are fiercely divided— Antebellum level divided— appearance is worse than reality. Though we may be more polarized today than we were in 2014, many Americans still want to sit in the middle, without wedding themselves to one of two extreme ideologies. They can be politically aware, ideologically independent, and encouraged to participate. There's room for everyone in this territory, and all that's needed is a perspective shift.

HOW PERSPECTIVES CAN BE CHANGED

A few years ago, I changed my own perspective. Instead of continuing to loyally follow mainstream media, I realized that the key to me feeling politically refreshed didn't require looking very far. Rather than orienting ourselves towards D.C., we can instead ground ourselves within our communities—focusing on political processes that operate on a more localized scale. I'm aware that this doesn't

---

Center's Journalism Project. Accessed October 11 2019. https://www.journalism.org/2014/10/21/political-polarization-media-habits/.

15 Ibid.

seem quite as exciting, but politics doesn't exist simply to entertain us. Awareness also applies: knowing how your tax dollars will be spent, what major projects are being undertaken in your town, and the ways in which *you* can play a part in affecting it. The people making decisions are always close-by, and the people affected by them are ourselves and our neighbors.

On the state and municipal levels, thousands tirelessly serve their communities. Whether through a volunteer opportunity or position as an elected official, their work often goes unnoticed. Someone can be a mayor, a member of the Zoning Board, or a mom collecting petition signatures opposing a new power plant. While so many of us are busy fighting over how best to solve the border crisis—despite our having no say in it at all—local politics is at work nearby, and you do have a say in it.Even though there can be drama, scandals, and partisan warfare (it's still politics after all), these political ills are generally less severe on local levels. Opponents know each other personally and are sometimes even friends. While Washington, D.C. is far removed from everyday American lives, state and municipal politics are firmly grounded in their communities. There's nowhere to hide, and the focus remains on tackling issues and serving constituents—without celebrity-like egos and poisonous media-provoked firestorms.

WHY TOWN COUNCIL MEETINGS ARE WORTH ATTENDING

The best way to truly recognize these forces is experiencing them firsthand. One remarkable quality of America's political structure is that wherever you are, you fall under a local government run for the area's residents, by the area's residents. At the end of the day, you are in a town, a county, and a state – all these things, as well as being part of a nation. Your local area, your hometown—these are the center of your political arena. At first, involving yourself locally may seem far less exciting than tuning into primetime cable news programs. However, once I got involved, I found ignoring the local was no longer an option.

HOW I USED TO BE

Between 2008 and 2016, I didn't miss a single presidential debate.

It didn't matter if it was primary contenders, major party nominees, or even vice-presidential picks. What mattered to me was having an opportunity to see politics in action, with those vying to govern engaged in battle. These events seemed so important that I had no issues rearranging my schedule to accommodate watching. Sometimes this meant doing homework early, reconfiguring social plans, or in one case, scrambling to make it to the nearest television during a family vacation. At the time, I lived in Glastonbury. Throughout all of this, I never once thought to give the town's political affairs any attention. Though my ears would perk up during midterm and general election seasons to hear who was running, most of what happened between cycles flew right by me. Being away at school certainly didn't help keep me engaged. As soon as I returned home, I felt it was time.

HOW THAT CHANGED

About a week after a post-graduation homecoming, I was scrolling through a Hartford Courant reporter's Twitter. Here I saw a posting about an upcoming Town Council meeting. Since I had never been to one before—and only knew of a few Council members—I felt compelled to go. After dinner on a rainy Tuesday evening, I made the five-minute commute to Town Hall, and casually meandered to the Council's chamber. In a town of over 30,000, only thirty residents were in attendance (which I later found out was considered high turnout). Among the thirty engaged citizens present, I was the youngest... by a few decades. The meeting's primary matter was the proposed construction of a major aquatic facility. Designed for competitive meets and recreational swimming, I initially thought it sounded great. After taking a few too many swims in the dire Glastonbury High School pool, the architectural mockups projected on-screen looked impressive. But, as the meeting progressed, it became evident that the project would cost the town around $15 million total to be completed. After some details were ironed out, the floor was completely open to the town's residents to address the Council directly.

Two elderly men approached the microphone and cited their opposition. Both were town residents since the 1970's and questioned the necessity of adding such a facility—especially at such a hefty price. The word "unnecessary" was thrown around, and each made a made a strong, fiscally-motivated case. Their comfort approaching the stand and presenting their case told me that this wasn't either's first rodeo.They were followed by a few women in favor of the project. One, an ex-competitive swimmer, presented the benefits of a local practice facility; the other touted the facility's therapeutic purposes for senior citizens and patients recovering from injuries. A substantial showing from high school swimmer parents also made a case for the project. While the first two men highlighted this ambitious project's non-necessity, these next individuals explained why it *is* necessary: for the health of our senior citizens, the athletic pursuits of our children, and the overall quality of our town. As I watched this unfold, I realized it wasn't quite what I'd expected.

My anticipation was for a heavily technical and bureaucratic discussion among officials; I was astonished by how easy it was for citizens to honestly speak directly to those in power. While it's difficult to even get through to staffers for congresspeople or senators, the floor was completely open at this meeting. Those who voiced their positions were town residents, exercising rights endowed to all of us. While not everyone feels so passionately about an aquatic facility, different issues invariably arise at each meeting, and some of them are bound to move us at some point.

Afterwards, the Council addressed a development company representative, after he'd cycled through a slideshow of proposals, mockups, and figures. With five Democrats and four Republicans seated beside each other, I anticipated significantly more conflict than there was. Members of each party echoed some of the same concerns, accepting the value that such a facility would have on the community but expressing skepticism over the cost, especially considering usage wouldn't be free despite tax dollars constructing it.

They asked similar questions to projects presenters, and conducted themselves civilly, as a wall of decision-makers aiming to protect the town's interests. Though I could not clearly distinguish proponents from opponents, conclusions didn't seem to be confined along party lines as they always seemed to be in Congress.

WHY THIS IS SIGNIFICANT

Once discussion concluded, the room emptied despite having an hour left to continue the meeting. As I lingered, digesting information, I watched the group trickle out—all maintaining the same opinions they had upon entry. Swim parents gathered in the hall looking over a petition, while the old men grumbled out together. A Councilman later told me, "the people who come to these meetings are the ones hell bent one way or the other." As someone without a prior opinion, I continued to ruminate on the merits and pitfalls of the plan. While adding another amenity to the town would boost desirability— especially after decades without a major project—is something for this purpose worth this cost? My mind was spinning. Had I not attended the meeting, I never would've given the project a second thought.

I heard that if both Town Council and Board of Finance were to approve the project, it may appear on the ballot come Election Day. Voting Glastonbury residents will get to select "Yes" or "No" on the matter. While it ended up not making it onto the ballot, attending this meeting made the complexities of the case clear; if I hadn't gone to this meeting and the question did appear on the ballot, chances are I would have made an uninformed Election Day decision. There have been a few referendums in the recent past: one was a renovation to the town's library, another related to the proposed construction a boathouse along the Connecticut River. I remember knowing what *names* to vote for, but being at a complete loss on if I should vote "Yes" or "No" to projects. I didn't know how the costs would impact taxes, or whether the project would increase the town's desirability. It was essentially a shot in the dark—one that I'm certain my friends and neighbors have taken in the past as well.

WHY ANYONE CAN AND SHOULD DO THIS

Glastonbury's residents will likely not be much impacted by who sits on the Supreme Court, what happens with the Mueller Investigation, or restrictions on southern state abortion rights. However, the pattern clear to me is that it's much easier to get politically invested in polarizing, emotionally-charged national issues than ones in our own backyards.

Glastonbury is thriving because of in-migration. It's strong school system, economic health, public safety, and aesthetic charm drive people to settle here, which provides a solid tax base to keep the town afloat. It's the job of town boards and commissions to keep this going, bearing in mind the best interest of all residents. Political awareness includes understanding the mechanisms operating, who is involved, and what can be done further. While it remains important to engage in national news, doing so at the expense of the local only breeds ignorance and division, distracting us from more tangible issues that affect us every day. Yes, local news exists—surprise, I watch it every morning. But politically, it only typically covers statewide issues. This includes how and what your governor's administration is doing (and how it affects you), and that's only one part of the package.

So much also occurs at local level, within your town or city. There's likely a local newspaper available, and a local-access television station, or community Facebook page (not yet tainted by profit-seeking partisans). While it's important to engage with all of these things, most can be gained by paying attention in-person.

HOW TO MAKE THE MOST OF FOLLOWING LOCAL POLITICS

Local political involvement can come in a number of flavors. Involvement can be physical and prompt one to run for office or volunteer; it can also be merely mental, resulting in increased literacy on local issues. Many opportunities for involvement exist and are absolutely underutilized. After attending this first meeting, I decided to make a habit of going. From a web search, I discovered that Glastonbury holds Town Council meetings on the first and third Tuesday of each month. I had seen notices for public hearings, posted around the town. In the past I'd have kept driving but have since started to stop and read. I've screenshotted tweets from local officials and reporters, announcing various municipal events.Now, going to local government meetings is my version of going to the movies.

Those close to me know about my intense aversion to movie theaters. Something about the darkness, noise, length, and smell makes me feel trapped, when I could simply watch the same movie a few months later for free in the comfort of my home. This leisure time has void been filled by council meetings and public hearings, and I feel they trump movies on a number of levels: Town Hall is much closer to my house than the nearest movie theater, the lights remain on the entire time, and there is no stigma against checking your phone Obviously, I am in a very small minority on this one. Most of my peers would unequivocally prefer going to see a movie, but the two are not mutually exclusive. Chances are, everyone is invested in at least some local issues, though perhaps miss opportunities to directly involve themselves.

Cue a public hearing over a proposed hotel on a vacant lot in town. The hotel would be a part of the rapidly expanding "AC Hotel by Marriot" chain, which espouses sleek, modern design in its locations. After an architect pitched the design—a hotel clad with silver paneling and a thirty-three percent glass facade—the discussion evolved into a wider debate about the town's architectural brand. As a quaint, New England community, many buildings in the town center stick to a traditionalist, brick-and-mortar design. As the councilmembers raised fears over how a "shiny, metal building" would fit in with the rest of town, one said something that really struck me:"

If we approve this, we'll never hear the end of it from members of the community."

Again, this was uttered at a public hearing—held specifically to provide a platform for community member concerns. About five of those community members were in attendance. Only one stood up to address the council directly with an opinion on the issue.

WHY REFOCUSING IS THE FIRST STEP

Politics is unavoidable. It operates everywhere, at every level, for every American. It's there every time you turn on the TV, open a newspaper, or check your phone. On the other hand, politics is also avoided. When it's not advertised (to sometimes nauseating degrees), it flies under the radar, requiring effort and action to notice and keep up with it. Rather than getting too sucked-in by what you read, or shying away from it completely, instead know where to look and what truly matters most. While mass media consistently dominates discourse, a lot can be gained in the local. Instead of cursing at the news or hurling insults on Facebook, get out of the house. Go to a campaign event, office hours with your representative, or a public hearing at the Town Hall. It's a lot easier when you treat it like going to the movies.

CHAPTER 3:

CELEBRATING THE MOST WONDERFUL TIME OF THE YEAR

"Who is the president?" There is a reason this question is asked to young children, forgetful seniors, and head-trauma patients. It's a piece of knowledge so ubiquitous that *not* knowing it entails a disconnect with the most basic levels of reality. Regardless of being a civic whiz or an apolitical avoidant, it's nearly certain that you can answer this fundamental question.

That said, substantially fewer Americans are able to identify their governor or senators—despite them being major officeholders in each state. What's far more concerning is that only forty-six percent of Americans know each state has two U.S. Senators.[16]

Ignorance only gets worse when the official in question is locally appointed, rather than statewide. In fact, according to a 2017 poll, only thirty-seven percent of Americans were able to name their U.S. Representative.[17] Only a select few can recall their State Senator, State Representative, or municipal officeholders—even though these officials are closest to their constituents. Many may not know or care that these positions even exist.

The aforementioned public servants can't and don't receive the same level of attention the president does, but that does not make them any less valuable. We are fortunate enough to live in nation with many tiers of representation, all of which are selected by our own votes; the first step to civic literacy is to understand what these roles are, how they're connected, and who fills them. Unaware individuals may mistakenly believe that Election Day is a Leap-Year-like phenomenon. Every four years the country comes to

16 Gintautas Dumcius. 2016. "Poll: Only 46 Percent Of Americans Know Each State Has Two U.S. Senators". Masslive. Accessed October 11 2019. https://www.masslive.com/politics/2016/03/edward_m_kennedy_institute_pol.html.

17 Nick Freiling. 2017. "Just 37% Of Americans Can Name Their Representative | Haven Insights". Haven Insights. Accessed October 11 2019. https://www.haveninsights.com/just-37-percent-name-representative/.

a screeching halt, all eyes on a map covered by two primary colors. However, those are just a quarter of all elections we have in America—the other three quarters are when the vast majority of our officials are selected. All of them deserve our attention, but with only twenty-seven percent of eligible voters participating in municipal elections, attention is obviously elsewhere.[18]

Some may attribute this troubling statistic to apathy for local politics, but I wouldn't go that far. Instead, I think most people haven't been up close and personal with it. Elections that have the highest turnouts are ones in which everyone knows who is running and why. Hillary vs. Trump, Obama vs. McCain, Bush vs. Gore—all turned both candidates into household names (if they weren't already). Even people with little interest in politics or knowledge about elections cannot avoid these paradigms, so they're more inclined to form judgments and vote. It's much harder to capture attention locally. There are races for myriad positions, including the ones that average people don't know about. Even if voters understand the governmental structures, they may still see a list of random names and party affiliations come Election Day. Those who do vote will largely base decisions on party

18   Zoltan Hajnal. 2018. "Opinion | Why Does No One Vote In Local Elections?". Nytimes.com. Accessed October 11 2019. https://www.nytimes.com/2018/10/22/opinion/why-does-no-one-vote-in-local-elections.html.

or which names they like most (this really happens). Many lack the initiative to go out and vote at all.

The best remedy for this is to cultivate an appreciation for the electoral process. This involves understanding who is running for what, and viewing races not as isolated occurrences but as specificities within larger trends. Once that's done, the first Tuesday in November becomes way more interesting.

WHY NOVEMBER IS THE NEW DECEMBER

Growing up, if you were to ask me what my favorite holiday was I wouldn't have had a unique answer. Call me basic, materialistic, or cliché—it was Christmas. For me, the beauty of Christmas wasn't in the holiday itself, but the entire season leading up. I mean, there's a reason it's so widely known as "the most wonderful time of the year."

Decorations displayed on every corner, festive programs airing on television, celebratory community events, and buzzing anticipation surrounding holiday surprises; joy and excitement on a yearly basis. Despite growing older and no longer receiving visits from Santa Claus, Christmas continues to be something I look forward to. Now, I enter Christmas-mode immediately after another holiday season ends; one that, despite conventional wisdom, offers its own festivities. I've even come to enjoy it more than Christmas.

My most wonderful time of the year is election season.

WHY THEY'RE NOT SO DIFFERENT FROM EACH OTHER

Instead of lit-up trees and ornamented wreaths, lawn signs and waving candidates decorate the streets. Rather than playing "Rudolph the Red-Nosed Reindeer" or "Elf," airwaves are flooded with polling results, campaign coverage, and—my personal favorite—candidate ads. Finally, rallies, town halls, and fundraisers are open to the public, like tree lightings and nativity pageants, all to bring communities together in holiday spirit.I still seem to be in the minority on this one. Voter turnout data comparing wealthy, developed countries consistently places the USA near the bottom, only beating out Japan and Switzerland.[19] In the 2012 presidential election, only 130.2 million Americans cast ballots out of the 241 million eligible.[20] With almost half of Americans not voting during general elections and less than half voting in midterm and municipal ones, the spirit of the season clearly hasn't moved enough people.

Imagine it's a week before Christmas and you get a knock on the door. You open it up, and a pack of cheerful carolers burst

---

19 Plumer, Brad. 2016. "Why 100 Million Americans Won't Vote On Tuesday". Vox. Accessed October 11 2019. https://www.vox.com/policy-and-politics/2016/11/7/13536198/election-day-americans-vote.

20 Ibid.

into a rendition of "Deck the Halls." If you don't know the song, care about the message, or plan to celebrate the holiday, of course you'll cut the interaction short. While this may sound cruel or misanthropic, it happens all the time when a candidate knocks on a door in the lead-up to Election Day. This citizen doesn't know who the candidate is, care about the issues, or plan to vote. Simply improving our understanding of who is running and why can drastically improve the road to Election Day: you'll recognize names and faces, you won't change the channel when a commercial comes on in order to evaluate it, and you may even consider stepping out of a bystander role to take action.

Awareness transforms election season from annoying to invigorating.

HOW I CAME TO HOLD THIS OPINION

Growing up, I always looked forward to Election Day. While I like to think I developed a penchant for civic engagement at a young age, it was actually because I got the day off from school. In my town and many others across the country, public schools are used as polling places, and—to this day—my elementary school is where my family and I cast our ballots.

I accompanied my parents to vote each year. There was something enthralling about meandering through the empty hallways I traversed each day, peeking through classroom windows only to see chairs up and lights off. The occasion overlapped our annual book sale, so the emptiness allowed private time with the most-frequented displays. My parents were always consistent voters, so Election Day was a yearly tradition to look forward to. I have memories of waiting in lengthy lines to reach the registration desk on general election years, walking past throngs of sign-wavers flashing the names of candidates for state-wide office during midterm election years, and entering a near-empty gymnasium on off-years when only municipal positions were voted on.

WHY JUST VOTING ISN'T ENOUGH

Despite weak voter turnout rates that plague our democracy, voting was a routine act in my household. Though my parents deserve praise for consistently participating, they nevertheless often did so rather blindly. Focusing their attention on the top-of-ticket races like president and governor, their down-ballot votes were typically cast along party lines, with very limited knowledge of who was running for what locally. While there's nothing wrong with supporting one party over another, I've learned that such an allegiance should not be used to justify stepping into the voting booth unprepared.

Understandably, I developed the same habits. Whenever the news was playing in the living room (which was often) or my father was engaged in a heated, political discussion with a friend or family member (which was also often), the focus was always national and never local. As adolescents, most of our political insights come straight from our parents. So—like them—I was politically engaged through high school, but in a limited capacity.

HOW I LEARNED THIS IN SCHOOL

Midterm election season in 2014; I was a senior in high school. One of the unique features of Glastonbury High School's curriculum is the course Current Issues (abbreviated CI), which all seniors are mandated to take. There is also only one section of CI each year, offered during first period, so all 500+ seniors are packed into the auditorium each morning, in an effort to prepare us for the lecture-driven courses we would encounter in college. Taught by eight history teachers who gave rotating lectures, units ranged from Ukraine to Ebola to ISIS to capture the moment's most pressing issues. To me, the unit that stood out most was one that started in late-October and concluded in early-November.

I bet you can guess what it was. Though we began the election unit with a discussion on national climate, focus quickly pivoted to the local level. The 2014 election was the first time many of my classmates were of voting age. In addition to posting voter registration tables outside the auditorium and steadfastly expressing the importance of voting to us, CI lecturers also educated us on our options. They invited both the Republican and Democratic candidates for State Representative and State Senate to give remarks and answer questions. For the first time, many of us were confronted face-to-face with the democratic process.

On that same day, we received a handout containing a flow-chart resembling a totem pole. It laid out all positions up for election on our local ballot, equipped with candidate photos and seat term limits. Governor topped the sheet, followed by U.S. Representative, then State Senator, lastly State Representative (the latter two I knew absolutely nothing about). Seventeen-year-old me latched on to the concisely constructed handout–while all of my materials from CI are long gone, I have yet to throw that sheet away.

Before this class, I'd heard the names and seen the faces of most of these candidates. Sometimes they were on a lawn sign, other times in the local newspaper. None of it meant very much to me, until I saw it all come together during CI.

HOW TO ACHIEVE THIS YOURSELF

Simply understanding who is running for what does wonders for one's political perspective. While the political world can seem confusing and complex—with myriad names and positions floating around—merely grasping the distinction between them helps demystify the entire election process. While my classmates and I were presented directly with this information, for most it involves specifically seeking it out. This does not mean hours spent filtering through policy proposals but can be as simple as familiarizing yourself with different levels of representation, searching for which districts your address is located within, and finding candidates for positions in state/local newspapers or online. Some places even release mock ballots in advance of Election Day, so voters can familiarize themselves with the layout and names beforehand. From there, simply searching the candidates will provide a solid biography–you'll have their appearance, party, position, and credentials under your belt. Another valuable thing to do is engage with a candidates' Facebook page right off the bat, regardless of whether you know or support them.

This allows for a steady consumption of campaign materials; you can see their pictures, watch their videos, and read their statements up to Election Day to ensure being as informed as possible before casting a vote.

It's also important to keep eyes peeled for candidate mentions and appearances. This way, if you decide you want to meet them, you know where and when to do it. The point is to so sufficiently acquaint yourself that there are no surprises or mysteries come Election Day. You'll reach a point where you feel like you know these candidates and have developed solid judgments beyond names and parties.

While some may deem candidate familiarization as a daunting, boring, or unimportant task, it represents the bare minimum we should carry with us to the polls. Think about why restaurants might include photos, descriptions, or translations on their menus: why select something if you don't know what you're getting? Though what you order for dinner may seem more important than State Capitol representation (and trust me, I often feel the same way), it definitely is not. Election season is long, and candidates are experts at putting themselves out there. A little bit of research will go a long way—you may find out you really love (or really *not* love) someone running.

WHY NOT ALL ELECTIONS ARE CREATED EQUAL

This acquaintance with your candidates serves as an excellent foundation of knowledge that every American voter should have. That said, there is a further layer of understanding to be cultivated: one espoused by the politically engaged themselves, who don't simply view the local election system in relation to names and faces, but in terms of strategies and trends. Once I realized the importance of cultivating such a foundation, I wasn't going to stop. Educating myself on local political matters showed me just how accessible it would be to play a part in them myself. I wanted to learn the ins-and-outs that allows political insiders to evaluate, predict, and discuss these matters. Fortunately for me, I had the privilege of meeting Chris Healy and hearing what he had to offer.

HOW I LEARNED THIS FROM AN EXPERT

One of my most vivid political memories is sitting in Chris Healy's office in 2016. Freshman year of college finished just days before, and I'd enthusiastically returned back to Connecticut for what I thought (at the time) was my first summer of adulthood. These feelings of maturity were reinforced by the fact that I—a fresh-faced 18 year-old in khakis—was attending a meeting at the imposing Legislative Office Building in Hartford. The last time I was there was during an elementary school field trip. Times had changed. Overwhelmed by the formality of my surroundings, Healy greeted me in the lobby. Even though I didn't realize then, this was the start of a new chapter of my life.

A veteran political operative and former chairman of the Connecticut GOP, Healy was working with Senate Republicans to turn enough blue districts red to secure a long-fought-for majority. As a total novice when it came to local politics, I listened intently while Healy pointed to a poster-sized map of Connecticut's thirty-six State Senate districts, rattling off a litany of facts and specific race details. In this moment, it was clear that Chris Healy was nothing short of an expert: understanding specific, competitive factors in each of these districts and knowing which political figures resided within them. I left that meeting feeling educated and inspired by Healy's words. Per this connection, I spent the summer working for Lorraine Marchetti, the Republican running for State Senate in my home district. As for Chris Healy—we kept in touch. In 2017, I returned to Connecticut prior to Election Day to help Healy canvas for Board of Education in his hometown Wethersfield. For me, he has remained an invaluable political connection ever since.

HOW HEALY SEES THINGS

In a coffee-shop conversation with Healy, he spoke about politics in a way I'd never heard before. Instead of relaying a first-person account of a campaign experience, Healy's decades of strategic, behind-the-scenes experience and deep understanding of Connecticut's political landscape allowed him to speak more generally about the process of running for office. He highlighted underlying commonalities between local races, visible to insiders but hidden to distracted laypeople. Particularly, he spoke about greater forces behind a successful run: respect to the candidate, the seat being competed for, and overall political climate.

Healy rendered the campaign process down to a simple analogy. "It's like a startup," he began, "and you need to sell it to investors by the roll out date." In this instance, the startup is the candidate, investors are voters, and roll out date is Election Day. The two "startups" are pitted against one another, courting the same investors, only one able to succeed in the end. Since this enthralling, high-stakes process repeats itself—cycle after cycle—people like Healy are able to view things more formulaically, similar to expert start-up investors. As I learned from him that day, his many insights are not closely guarded secrets.

WHY SO MUCH IS DETERMINED BY THE CANDIDATES

While the phrase "anyone can run for office" is true, it's not so cut-and-dry when it comes to *successfully* running for office. Healy emphasized that winning elections is all about, "finding the right candidate, at the right time, with the right support." When I first heard this, I was most perplexed by the notion of a "right candidate." It seemed to me that a candidate's rightness was contingent upon factors specific to their individual race. From the perspective of a seasoned party operative, however, certain traits give candidates an edge when thrown to competitive campaign battlefields. The type of candidate Healy alluded to is fresh, motivated, and cautious. While a "15-year town selectman" will be experienced, established, and no stranger to government service, this candidate can be too complacent, and often overestimates their name recognition and popularity. As a result, their campaign is seldom aggressive or captivating enough for voters. He also stressed the importance of not underestimating a candidate's long-term viability. While he's interested in how someone will do in the current field, things don't just end after a win.

Things may start locally, but for many, there will be re-election campaigns and opportunities to seek higher office. "Candidates are most viable before their third term," he stated, alluding to the danger of political stagnation. To demonstrate this point, Healy cited two of Connecticut's greatest political success stories: Former Governor John Rowland and Senator Chris Murphy. Both of these figures scaled the political latter through strategic escalation from local to statewide office. Rowland was elected to the State House at age twenty-three, served two terms before being elected to the US House, and ran for governor after serving two terms in Washington. Murphy served two terms in the State House, two in the State Senate, and three terms in the US House, before getting elected to the US Senate. Through this incremental and timely advancement, Rowland and Murphy preserved their political appetites, never staying put long enough to get too comfortable. They were able to maintain the moniker "Rising Star." As soon as their particular seat got too comfy, these two jumped to pursue bigger things before it was too late. According to Healy, a strong candidate is hungry and on-guard.

WHY THE SEAT MATTERS TOO

Candidate strength is not the only factor that matters when evaluating elections. Not all elections are created equal, but Healy explained that all *can* be placed into one of two categories. "There are two different animals," he started, "the challenged seat and the open seat," each with their own set of pros and cons. The type of race a candidate enters is integral to determining their path to success. In a challenged seat race, one candidate races against an incumbent, who will typically have the advantage of name recognition on their side. Healy enumerated three consecutive steps a candidate must take to defeat an incumbent.

First, the candidate must raise doubt about the incumbent, generally through leveraging some position, vote, or view of theirs to make a case against them.Once there is enough discontent surrounding the incumbent, the candidate may proceed to the *second step*: the introduction of an alternative. Platform is key here, because it must be presented to the voters by the candidate in a palatable form, to clarify their position against the incumbent.*Finally,* the candidate must drive enthusiasm for their own candidacy. They must inspire and capture voters' emotions to rally enough enthusiasm to cast a vote for them. Merely getting voters to agree is not sufficient; it is fierce, dedicated campaigning that drives action. Cue the pictures reading to elementary schoolers, videos walking around with rolled-up sleeves at a county fair, speeches, mailers, and door-to-door visits.

When seeking an open seat, there is no incumbent advantage. Though this may seem like an advantage, when the incumbent is removed from the equation, so is the tangible target a candidate can focus on. According to Healy, the key in an open race is to analyze the constituency to determine ad target who can best be won over. Healy noted that, "When an incumbent controls a district for term after term, people stop paying attention." Therefore, it's up to the candidate to research past voting trends and participation levels to strategically carve out a pursuable voting bloc. While vying for a challenged seat, the candidate must rally voters against the incumbent; when the seat is open, the candidate must start from scratch and build a voter coalition to rally around them.

HOW THE NATIONAL CLIMATE AFFECTS IT ALL

Though national politics should certainly be evaluated separately from what happens on state and local levels, its monstrous prevalence tends to trickle down, impacting voter patterns even on unrelated matters. When it seems like a strong local candidate is running a winnable race, the political mood on a national level nevertheless has a profound impact. This can be frustrating and unfortunate for candidates who face a major disadvantage for reasons beyond their control, but alternatively, this phenomenon can be a great help to others.

In 2018, Connecticut Republicans found this out the hard way. After two terms of a Democrat governor—whose approval ratings dropped to seventeen percent cross-state by his tenure's end—Republicans thought it was their time to finally reclaim the position. Unfortunately, despite touting a platform that would eliminate income tax and block implementation of state highway tolls, Democrats claimed yet another victory even though they ran an objectively weak campaign. According to Healy, this is because "Democrats found and communicated with voters with a visceral hatred of Trump." The odds were against Connecticut Democrats, considering their unpopular leadership. This, however, that was no match for the "Blue Wave," which tremendously boosted their candidates across all levels. When evaluating when to run, candidates must absolutely take into account national climate.

I view this as an unfortunate byproduct of our fixation with national politics. In actuality, local politics is so removed from national politics, but voting habits tell a different story. While candidates must expect it and deal with it today, this problem can be ameliorated if more people go local.

WHY THIS WILL CHANGE THE WAY YOU VIEW ELECTIONS

By the end of this conversation, I could see politics work from Healy's perspective. While a candidate or campaign manager can provide a detailed, first-person account of a race, Healy's tenure as a top party official gave him the ability to speak about elections from a top-down perspective. His involvement with so many races over the years has put him in-tune with the general framework and driving factors of a successful campaign. Voters who understand the election system are akin to educated consumers seeing advertisements. Both are aware of the end goal and recognize that their support is integral to attain it. Understanding this more complex layer of local elections allows us to no longer be victims to the system. We can better recognize the strategies candidates and campaigns employ and grasp how and why they do it. Not only does this allow for greater liberty come Election Day, it also endows powerful campaign skills.

These considerations come second-nature to people like Chris Healy. Though they seemed complex to me at first, they are now the first things I think about when I look at a new race. Mastering these fundamentals can allow anyone to look at any campaign, recognize its strengths and weaknesses, and establish its best route forward.

The best way to do this is simply to pay more attention. More closely observe races happening around you, to see what's working and what isn't. Read up on local history to draw parallels with what's happening in the present. Finally, involve yourself and meet people in political circles with stories, insights, and lessons just like these. While Chris Healy may be Connecticut's resident Republican expert, other states and parties have their own superstars to pass along wisdom.

When I think back to meeting with Healy, I realize that he considered all of these conditions overseeing Republican campaigns for State Senate across Connecticut, to ensure that viable candidates ran. It's no wonder Republican candidates for State Senate had a particularly strong showing that year!

While we'll often see hard work done by those on-the-ground in the late stages of a campaign, expertise from those at the top can be a powerful, strategic force. Though invisible to the public eye, it should not be ignored.It takes time and effort to fully understand politics on a local level as a spectator. However, this is worth your investment. Whether it entails learning candidate names or uncovering strategic forces that contribute to a campaign's success, it's not too difficult. Perhaps once you've got a true taste of politics, you'll want more.

Watch out, Christmas.

CHAPTER 4:

SHEDDING LIGHT ON POLITICAL FIGURES

———

We have a tendency to overinflate the status of celebrities. I realized this when I was just a few years old and a Disney Channel star sat at the table beside me in a Florida deli. At first, I was in disbelief. How was this famous, *Lizzy McGuire* actor dining in the same restaurant as my family and me? Wouldn't he have his meals hand-prepared by a personal chef while flying aboard a private jet?In reality, he was just a young guy, who acted for a living, with a taste for pastrami.

WHY WE CONFLATE POLITICIANS AND CELEBRITIES

When we constantly see someone on TV or in the news, it's easy to forget that they exist outside of those platforms. When we dehumanize celebrities this way, it can make for some awkward encounters (like excessive staring while said celebrity tries to eat his sandwich in peace) that perpetuate the perceived gap between us and them. For better or worse, celebrities are not limited to actors, musicians, or television and internet personalities. In fact, anyone with widespread recognition is a celebrity in their own right. Whether it's a high-profile senator frequently featured on primetime news programs or a small town mayor sure to attend every ribbon-cutting ceremony, elected officials are subject to the public eye's scrutiny, same as Hollywood stars.

HOW THEY CAN LOOK ALIKE

Occasionally, politicians receive the same esteem other celebrities do if their message and personality generate enough fandom. Historically, political success has been contingent on cultivating group support, particularly in the form of product branding. Dwight Eisenhower's "I Like Ike" merchandise helped win the presidency by literally plastering his childhood nickname on thousands of American chests. This sounds familiar to "Beto" gear now sported by thousands of Americans—in Texas and beyond—during O'Rourke's

2018 Senate campaign.Then, there's fame derived from media superstardom. Whether it's Bill Clinton playing his saxophone on *The Arsenio Hall Show* or Alexandria Ocasio-Cortez's social media use to rise from first-term, New York Congresswoman to national voice of the progressive movement—some politicians directly take a page out of the celebrity playbook.

Finally, there are those utilizing both tactics, like a certain red-hat-wearing, twitter-using Celebrity-in-Chief.More often than not, political fame looks more like infamy. Politics is inherently controversial. Campaigns are competitions; serving as an elected official is walking on a tightrope, trying to balance the interests of all groups affected. The more fervent a politician's fanbase is, the stauncher their opponents will be. It's just part of being in the spotlight.

Because of our political system's increasingly partisan nature, media coverage thrives on drama. At the dramatic center are those in power: constantly blamed by the public for disagreeing with our own views or making decisions we don't like.

WHY THIS ISN'T ALWAYS A GOOD THING

Considering all of this, it's sometimes difficult to remember that politicians are not super-humans; they are not fictional characters created by cable news executives to boost viewership. Though some exploit their celebrity status more than others, most are primarily concerned with doing their jobs.

The best of them are most concerned with doing their jobs well.

Politicians are people who hold jobs that require being in the public eye. This airtime is necessary for ideological purposes—we can evaluate what they've accomplished, to determine if their employment contract should be extended. That said, we can get carried away: forgetting that beneath the headlines, snippets, and memes sits a person, just like you and I, doing a job. There are also droves of politicians without any star power, elected at a local level and serving a small population. Our relationship with these figures is harmed by celebritization: we pay less attention to locals, while obsessing over national profiles (even if they don't even represent us). Social division between politicians and citizens contributes to partisanship, disengagement, and cynicism. The best way to close these gaps is with personal connection.

While your senator may be difficult to sit down with, local and state officials lead normal lives in normal places. They don't travel with a pack of secret service agents, or only communicate with a chief-of-staff; they *do* make themselves accessible to their constituents.Local political involvement bridges the gap between public and private citizens. You can work alongside them on a campaign, talk with them at events, and get to know them beyond their name, title, and hyper-posed headshot.Politicians are people too, after all.

WHY POLITICIANS ARE LIKE AMERICAN IDOL CONTESTANTS

When I was younger, I watched no show as religiously as American Idol. Based on the conversations I continue to have about it with fellow viewers, I know I wasn't alone. Over the 2000's the show was a staple in most US households, airing twice a week and attracting millions of viewers—making it America's most watched reality show. Consistently attracting Americans of all demographics, American Idol brought people together to watch and participate in creating the next pop sensation.

The show's premise was simple. Each year, crowds of fifteen to twenty-eight-year-old Americans filled stadiums across the country for a chance to audition before a panel of judges. If most judges supported them, off they'd go to Hollywood. The top twenty-four contestants then performed on live TV. After every performance, judges would give their feedback, but it was ultimately up to the American people vote by phone after each show. After weekly eliminations, one contestant emerges victorious, the next American Idol. Obviously, they are not entirely equivalent, but American Idol is a lot like American politics. Contestants are candidates, competing for a certain position. Judges are commentators, constantly chirping-in with their views, but ultimately without the power to make any calls. And the voters are, well, the voters.

HOW BOTH START OUT AS NORMAL PEOPLE

Much of American Idol's appeal stemmed from its ordinary citizen contestants, sharing a common desire for musical stardom. When we watched a humble farmgirl—Carrie Underwood—nervously walk into the audition room in 2004, there was no way to know she would go on to win and become one of the most prolific country music artists of her generation. As the season progressed, viewers witnessed this remarkable progression from "average girl" to extraordinary celebrity. When politicians eventually emerge into the celebrity sphere, their humble roots seem like a thing of the distant past. Sure, when they first campaign they'll reference their upbringing, hardships, and personal lives, but once they're elected it's as if they're in a category of their own.

For example, prior to taking the political plunge, Sarah Palin worked for her husband's commercial fishing business. Cory Booker was a lawyer at a non-profit. As we heard time and again in 2008, President Barack Obama was a community organizer. Though these three have become household names—easily identifiable if seen passing by us on the street—they used to be regular people. Just as regular people on American Idol auditioned with the hopes of rising to stardom, these three citizens embarked on an audition of their own, ultimately leading them to their own stardom: running for office.

While American Idol viewers are able to witness a months-long transformation, political ascent takes much longer and is much less visible. This prompts us to lose sight of the politician's roots, and regard them instead as celebrities.

HOW EVEN HOUSEHOLD NAMES HAD FIRST AUDITIONS

Where you may see an iconic governor, a popular senator, and a universally known president, I see an Alaskan city councilwoman, a New Jersey City mayor, and a member of the Illinois State Senate. Although they've come to hold these prestigious titles, all started out as "normal" Americans, looking to serve their communities as local elected officials.

Across the country, there are thousands of others just like them. These people work in Washington D.C., a State Capitol, or a Town Hall. Though they lack the same name recognition as Palin, Booker, and Obama, the work they do is just as meaningful. That's why an integral component of understanding politics involves viewing politicians exactly as what they are: people. When it comes to local politics, this is much easier to see. Since most positions only demand part-time job commitment, officials' careers and lives can still go on relatively normally. In Glastonbury, three of our longest serving Town Councilmen simultaneously worked as a veterinarian, a firefighter, and a real estate broker. Our longtime State Representative was a practicing allergist, continuing to see patients during his tenure.When we really look at these individuals, residing in our communities, shopping at our grocery stores, and trying to make a living for themselves and their families, they appear so similar to us. That said, they're still politicians too.

Not all politicians ship-off to Washington, trade in modest garb for a designer wardrobe, and have their faces broadcasted on national television. The sooner we realize that, the better.

WHY OUR RELATIONSHIP WITH POLITICS DEPENDS ON OUR RELATIONSHIP WITH POLITICIANS

A fundamental component of improving our relationship with politics involves improving our relationship with politicians. One piece of this is giving local politicians deserved recognition: learn who they are, get to know them personally, and respect their decision to serve.

The other piece surrounds non-local politicians, buzzing around Capitol Hill. Rather than demonizing these representatives for voting a certain way or criticizing them as "out of touch" or corrupt, take a look into who they were *before* assuming civic celebrity status. While some deserve this reputation, not everyone in Washington is Frank Underwood.

Media partisanship dehumanizes America's politicians, but it also creates distance between our political institutions and ourselves, dividing us into closed-off, ideological echo chambers. It's remarkable that *any* American can take office. You don't need royal blood or a dictator's appointment. Every politician starts out as a private citizen who makes a decision, and that decision is usually a local one.

HOW TO SEE BEHIND THE VEIL

Through campaign work and getting involved in local politics, I've seen behind the curtain that many believe separates "us" from "them." When a local candidate runs for office, the unengaged will see a few things: lawn sign campaign logos, a thirty second introduction clips, or newspaper op-eds endorsing (or criticizing) them. Sometimes the reception is positive. At their best, these campaign materials turn bystanders into supporters. Other times, voters will only see yet another name, on yet another sign, in yet another year. An impersonal acquaintance like this is not likely to spark a connection. However, there is so much more to these people, if both politicians and civilians try to bridge this gap.During campaign work over the years, I've interacted with political figures behind-the-scenes. This doesn't just mean ruminating in closed-door meetings about opposition research. More often than not, it was playing fetch with their dogs, hearing stories about their children's college experiences, and having personal conversations with them over long car rides. One time I even had to drive my candidate's car to a campaign stop—I was a nervous wreck the entire time! Most importantly, I've directly and candidly learned what these people are like and how they found their way to politics—things that aren't apparent to most voters.

WHAT CATHERINE TAUGHT ME

I first met Catherine Marx right before working on a campaign under her management. Upfront, I learned a few things about her: she was formerly Vice Chair of the Connecticut Republican Party, with tremendous competency, expert intuitions, and a massive network that allowed her to masterfully navigate the ins-and-outs of running a statewide campaign. After weeks of filtering through pictures at her kitchen table and traveling across the state to capture campaign footage, I came to know her personally as well. In addition to her exhaustive list of political credentials, she's a mother of three who drinks iced tea, plays tennis, and loves gardening.In a post-campaign conversation, she shared an insight with me that helped shape my political perspective. She told me, "Every politician's career begins when a lightbulb goes off in a private citizen's head telling him or her to do it."

HOW "LIGHTBULB MOMENTS" WORK

Catherine Marx experienced her "lightbulb moment" after she and her family had moved to Hebron, Connecticut. At the time, the big issue facing the town was the implementation of sidewalks—a project seeming relatively insignificant from afar but tied to many complicated financial, safety, and logistical concerns. When this mother of three found a flyer in her mailbox advertising a public hearing on sidewalks, the cause compelled her to attend. This was her first foray into local politics. Ultimately, she was inspired to expand her involvement in Hebron's Republican Town Committee, ultimately running for State Senate herself in 2004. Many others experience their "lightbulb moments" after taking action for a cause. These lightbulb moments mark the commencement of every political career, and can be triggered by anything at any time.

"Look at Thad," she started (referencing Thad Gray, whose campaign we met on), "his lightbulb moment came when he was told he should run." In Thad's case, his private sector Chief Investment Officer job provided him with significant experience, and a friend realized that he could use it manage the state's finances as Treasurer. The source of his lightbulb moment informed much of his candidacy: he was reserved, careful, and competent on the campaign trail, a departure from the boisterous, attention-craving behavior we often see. Understanding his motivation— someone else's suggestion on the basis of professional qualifications—explained so much about him as a person and his offerings as candidate.

Sometimes family members trigger "lightbulbs moments." Whether your father was a local selectman or President George H.W. Bush, experiencing the political world first-hand from a young age has enabled many to follow that path. These political legacies possess the advantage of professional connections and awareness of what political life entails. Sometimes, the lightbulb comes on in childhood, when— amidst a classroom full of aspiring astronauts and soccer players—a kid decides they want to be president (I know what you're thinking, but this wasn't me—I wanted to be a spy). This relates to the celebrity perception we have of our top political figures. From a child's point of view, the president is a real-life movie star-type, appearing on television, internet, and in newspapers daily, known by everyone in the country.Many adolescent presidential-hopefuls lose this desire, but for some the dream only intensifies. Catherine shared a story she'd heard of a sharp-talking, suit-donning Villanova student walking into class on his first day. When asked by a classmate, "Why are you wearing a suit?" his response was, "I'm going to be president someday." While he didn't make it to the presidency, this student was John Rowland, who went on to become Governor of Connecticut. Experiencing the lightbulb moment at such a young age gives time to decide what they want to aim for and devise a plan for how to get there.

For a few, these lightbulbs go off for the wrong reasons. They aspire to enter politics to fulfill self-serving ends like fame or money. A closer look beneath a politician's public façade, however, can and will reveal their intentions. By looking them up, reading their bios, and talking to them directly, we as voters can be more in touch with our politician's personal sides—even if they're not all positive. They may be wrapped up in scandal, responsible for dangerous legislation, or untrustworthy and incompetent. Still, personal acquaintance can help us realize these things firsthand and guide our voting patterns. Someone like this may belong to the party you align with, so without knowing their personalities you may end up supporting a party-line vote.

WHY "LIGHTBULB MOMENTS" HELP

On the national level, we know the personality before the person. These figures are introduced into our lives as a larger-than-life persona, far removed from ourselves. Surrounded by security personnel and a press flurry, it's immensely difficult for private citizens to relate to someone so seemingly removed from ordinary life. On the local level, it's a whole different ballgame.

The local political class is comprised entirely of people like you and I. They don't want to be gawked at. They don't want to be berated for supporting something you don't. But for the most part, they *do* want to develop positive relationships with constituents, even ones who disagree.Nowadays, it can be difficult not to automatically see politicians as corrupt, disingenuous, and self-serving. With attention focused on matters like Mitch McConnell's obstructionism or Hillary Clinton's emails, it's not surprising that the dark underbelly of politics stands out more in our minds.

When this trickles down, it impacts our perceptions of less visible politicians on the state and local levels. Ultimately, it breeds the dangerous consequences of fanaticism and retreat that were discussed in depth earlier.

HOW THIS GAP CAN BE CLOSED

Fortunately, our physical proximity to these figures allows for clearing this misconception if the right steps are taken. Most letters to the president receive no response, and contacting your senator or governor is difficult, especially if you don't like getting a busy signal (though for those of us who grew up casting American Idol votes, we're used to how that feels).

Thankfully, it's significantly easier to reach your local officials. In fact, it's usually as easy as going up to them and introducing yourself. With smaller constituent populations, the demand to talk to them is not particularly high. Thus, many avenues exist that allow for a relationship to be built. These include:

- Attend meet-and-greets, events, and office hours. Both on and off the campaign trail, candidates and sitting officials hold these within their districts to gain face-time with constituents in a casual setting. Often under-attended, they are great opportunities to tear down the wall between representative and constituent.
- Participate in municipal meetings. Town and city governments often receive little attention from their residents, despite the interactive nature of their meetings. In many instances, citizens can go up to a podium and directly address mayors, councilmembers, and aldermen regarding issues in a surprisingly informal fashion.
- Volunteer or run. No better way to erase boundaries between laypeople and politicians than entering civic domains firsthand. There are surprisingly few barriers to entry, and anyone is welcome to contribute as much or as little as they want to a candidate, party, or cause.

As I've come to realize through civic action, this behind – the-scenes experience transforms your political perspective. Rather than only seeing a politician's highly curated public persona, you come to understand everything that exists around that. You'll go to their house, meet their family, and learn far more about them than their professional credentials and ideological positions. It's the ultimate form of humanization.

WHY POLITICAL FIGURES NEED TO CONTRIBUTE TOO

The burden is not entirely on the voter though. To heal the divide, it's also up to politicians to reach out and make themselves accessible to constituents. As later chapters detail, local campaigning affords the ability to connect with voters on the ground: door-knocking, community events, and even waving on the side of the street. When face-to-face contact isn't an option, video can be unleashed to similar effect. Seeing and hearing a candidate make a video statement is significantly more impactful than reading the same statement while staring at a stiff headshot. There's a reason why television viewers of the 1960 Presidential Debate declared the cool and collected Kennedy winner over nervous, sweaty Nixon while radio listeners decided otherwise. Elected officials can stay down-to-earth by connecting with constituents after election season ends. Some, but not all, will host and attend events solely to listen to what people want and get to know them. Social media is also a revolutionary tool that allows politicians to keep followers posted on whereabouts and agendas. It also gives followers the opportunity to comment and message that continue the chain of communication between those representing and those being represented.

WHY WE'RE ALL BETTER OFF WHEN THIS HAPPENS

Though many look like celebrities, politicians are just people above all else. They're people who experienced lightbulb moments, took real action, and now are endowed with real power to serve other Americans. Some of them do this in the nation's capital; others do so in small towns. Who they are, why they are there, and what they do should be known to their constituents. The stronger our connection with elected officials, the healthier our democracy is. In an ideal world, this would mean cultivating stronger relationships with *all* of them. Realistically, though, this is a local issue. Don't just look down and shuffle past when you see a starry-eyed candidate passing out palm cards at the county fair. Take one and actually read it, search their name online, or go ask them why they're running for office. At worst, you'll lose a few minutes and know who not to vote for. At best, you'll become a supporter, volunteer with their campaign, and maybe even experience a lightbulb moment of your own.

CHAPTER 5:

PUTTING COMMUNITY ABOVE POLITICS

———

Politics is exciting—at least, *I* think it is. Over the past few chapters, I've listed things get me politically pumped, from scoring a front row seat at a public hearing to the smell of Election Day in the air. That said, I do realize that few share my excitement. If they did, I probably wouldn't be writing this book.

The reality is, many Americans aren't all that excited about politics. That doesn't mean they don't understand politics. It also doesn't mean they don't have political views; it doesn't even mean that they don't vote. What it does mean is a general lack of enthusiasm propelling people to get more directly involved. Now, I can explain the importance of Town

Council meetings, but I can't make anyone attend them (not even my family members). I can shed light on how elections work, but I can't make anyone pay attention. I can try to humanize politicians, but I can't make anyone go meet them.

If these chapters have instilled within you a new understanding of politics, they still may not have motivated you to do anything. As this book's first section comes to a conclusion, its focus will shift from *why* to get involved to *how* to get involved. If you're still not sold and find politics unexciting, I'll make one final case that may even appeal to politics' biggest haters.

WHY LOCAL POLITICS IS DIFFERENT

Since the beginning of this chapter, I've used the word "politics" (in some form) nine times. This was not by accident.

Politics is something that inherently turns some people off. Whether they view it as a necessary evil, great divider, or corrupt institution, it can be hard to convince them otherwise. This book, though, isn't just about politics. It's about local politics. Even if the political element seems off-putting, focusing on the local element can open this world up to otherwise disinterested demographics. Earlier chapters centered on refocusing our political sights to foreground the local, while placing national politics in the background.

However, there are those of us whose political sights aren't set anywhere. Even if your eyes are open, chances are you have a friend or family member whose aren't. Instead of accepting this demographic as a lost cause, they can be engaged by highlighting the components of local politics that are not heavily political.Once you look past party affiliations, policy views, and heated sparring that envelops politics at all levels, one thing always remains: a community.

HOW THIS WORKS ON A NATIONAL SCALE

Presidents represent the vast community that is the United States of America, and their platforms typically reflect how they lead. From Barack Obama's "Hope" to Donald Trump's "Make America Great Again," these slogans essentially sum up the message, goal, and tone of each administration. However. because the president represents the entire country, it's impossible to fully please. There will invariably be some people, from some demographics, in some places that don't see much hope or don't want America going back to the way it was again. Such variation is inevitable considering this country's extreme diversity. People in Wyoming lead very different lives than people in Brooklyn, and a leader cannot truly represent both communities equally well.

Representation is much more plausible on the local level, where leaders interact with individual cities, towns, and neighborhoods—all of which we undoubtedly recognize as communities.

WHY THIS IS STRONGER ON A LOCAL SCALE

Though many people dislike politics, few dislike their communities.Some of us are community-oriented because we've lived our entire lives within one. Other times, we're new community members after a recent move. Often, we have a lot in common with our fellow community members. We go to the same schools, eat at the same restaurants, and are affected by the same problems. We may have ethnic or socioeconomic similarities, we may live in the same kinds of houses, we may even work at the same businesses. Even if we disagree politically, we have an appreciation for the shared space we call home. Local politics is a great strengthener of this ideal.

Though politics can and will produce controversy and disagreement, its main purpose is leadership. That leadership shouldn't discriminate, isolate, or alienate. Local leadership should be accessible, visible, and universal—its primary purpose, after all, is to serve and represent a community. That's something anyone can get excited about.

WHY WAVING CAN MAKE WAVES

When I was in middle school, I witnessed a political phenomenon take Glastonbury by storm. It wasn't because of
a policy, project, or party. It was because a specific person
ran for office and demonstrated his commitment to the community. As a result, people across the political spectrum, of
varying levels of political involvement (and of all ages) got
excited about local politics.

HOW LOCAL POLITICS RATTLED THE SCHOOL BUS

The year 2010: I was in 8th grade and rode the bus to school
every day. If you've ever taken a middle school bus, you know
that while the afternoon ride is dominated by petty gossip
and inappropriate humor, during the morning ride everyone
is usually half-asleep. At about eight am each day, my bus
would stop at the intersection of New London Turnpike and
Oak Street. The stop had a perfect view of the monolithic Stop
and Shop—one of the town's vital organs pumping a constant circulation of suburban moms. Usually no one thought
anything of passing this corner.

One early autumn day this intersection was busier than usual.
There were no more cars on the road, but a group of figures
donning red shirts occupied the sidewalk in front of the
supermarket.On inspection, some of the signs read, "Prasad
Srinivasan for State Representative." As we all crowded the

windows to get a better look, one of my classmates recognized Srinivasan as his allergist. After returning home, I raced onto my iPod Touch to research. I found that the local, well-regarded doctor with no prior political experience was challenging an incumbent Democrat for the 31st District seat, covering almost all of Glastonbury. I was pretty intrigued, mostly because I had only seen political candidates in front of crowds on TV.

While local politicians surely existed, I had never seen one before. I didn't know any of their names, and I never particularly cared enough to learn. Each morning leading up to Election Day, the grinning Srinivasan would station himself on this busy corner and wave at hundreds of rush hour commuters passing by, as a way of acquainting them with him and his candidacy. Some days, he was alone. Other days, he had company. While he was sometimes accompanied by local Republicans, Srinivasan was most often joined by personal friends, who came out in droves to help. The next time we drove by, most of us crowded over to the windows, except this time, we remembered Srinivasan and knew what he was doing. Suddenly, a surge of positive energy swept over the bus, as over two dozen thirteen-year-olds waved, cheered, and ignored the bus driver's instructions to sit back down.

WHY APPEALING TO COMMUNITY MADE THIS HAPPEN

At the time, I found it odd that a group of mostly apathetic middle schoolers could respond so enthusiastically to a State Representative candidate—especially when no one even knew what a State Representative was. It could have been that Srinivasan's energy enlivened the gloomy morning routine. It could have been a matter of following the pack; after all, no one wants to be the only person on the bus not waving. For me, it was that this was my first time seeing politics in action. Direct campaigning, within my home domain. Though I was not yet of voting age, simply waving back felt like participation to me.Morning after morning, my bus would pass what we nicknamed "Prasad's Corner." As soon as the Stop and Shop came into sight, we'd flock to one side of the bus, roll down the windows, and wave and cheer for the same ten seconds every day. Srinivasan's smile would widen as he and his teammates waved back as we passed by. Our enthusiasm signaled to the Srinivasan team that their efforts were working. At school, classmates from other buses would discuss Srinivasan's presence. Some would even express disappointment at missing out on their route.

We could neither vote nor recount any policy positions, yet our adolescent attention spans were captured by something we'd never have expected.Fortunately, Srinivasan's appeal extended well beyond our demographic; adults on both sides of the aisle appreciated his positive energy during their

weekday commute. Soon, Prasad became a local phenomenon, despite many not even knowing what he was running
for and against. He brightened everyone's day with jubilance,
and demonstrated political qualification through showing
commitment, dedication, and vitality over time. Glastonbury
was proud to have the shared experience of waving to Prasad.
Their voting patterns prove so.

HOW THIS CAN CHANGE POLITICS AS WE KNOW IT

In 2010, Srinivasan flipped the district with fifty-six percent
of the vote. After, he won re-election three times—all by contributing a rational, bipartisan attitude to the General Assembly. During his terms he maintained an active local presence
and continued to practice medicine during his service. Over
a four-term tenure, his popularity only increased.In 2018, Srinivasan decided to run for Governor of Connecticut, but was
unable to cinch the nomination within a crowded field. However, his nomination speech—given by Glastonbury Republican Town Committee Chairman, John Tanski—highlighted
something remarkable. "In 2016, Glastonbury supported Hillary Clinton, Dick Blumenthal and John Larson," Tanski cited,
highlighting that Democratic candidates for President, U.S.
Senate, and U.S. Congress won within town. He continued,
"but an even larger majority, 70%, voted for Prasad."[21]

---

21 "Glastonbury RTC Chair John Tanski Nominates Rep. Prasad Sri-
    nivasan For Governor". 2019. Youtube. Accessed October 11 2019.

He was primarily regarded not as a Republican politician, but rather, a Glastonbury politician. Seeing Srinivasan's rise firsthand, it was evident that his community-driven campaign contributed to resounding success. As a doctor entering the political world for the first time, Prasad's constant sign-waving and cheerful personality turned him from an unglamorous state office candidate into a revered household name, simply by being *present*. He embodied what a local leader should be: someone the community knows, trusts, and can run into on the sidewalk.

That is why, when managing a campaign, myself, I made certain that our team waved as much as we possibly could, in as many locations as we possibly could. While the team of municipal candidates could not achieve the same stardom as the individual Srinivasan, through dedicated commitment we hoped to at least achieve the same recognition.

As cars whizzed by on the frigid mornings and windy evenings, I realized that for most drivers, this would be the only second of their days they would spend thinking about an election coming up. For that reason, I enjoyed doing it immensely, treating it as a friendly reminder. Hopefully, they remember come Election Day, and support those dedicated enough to spend hours waving on street corners.

---

https://www.youtube.com/watch?v=s76oHSNIxtk.

Oh, and every time a school bus drove by, I made sure to crank up my enthusiasm level and wave like crazy. You never know who you're going to inspire.

WHY LOCAL LEADERSHIP SHOULDN'T PICK SIDES

This community-centric approach to local leadership doesn't just evaporate after Election Day. While campaigns signify a rally for support, that support must then be held onto in office. For Prasad Srinivasan, this involved representing the people of Glastonbury in the Legislative Chambers of the State Capitol in Hartford. In other instances, political officials lead from within, totally immersed in the communities in which they reside.

One of these leaders is Jay Moran, mayor of Manchester, Connecticut. Located right next to Glastonbury, it's a town I've had a lot of contact with over the years. It's where my mother grew up, where my grandparents resided, and as of 2018, the home of my local Trader Joes.

The first thing I learned about Jay Moran was that he's the father of my neighbor's nanny (connections like this are not uncommon in local communities). Beyond that, Moran is the leader of the city's elected Board of Directors. However, first and foremost, he's a proud Manchester resident.

That pride is evident at every appearance he makes, every speech he gives, and every constituent conversation he has. He brings to the job an unbridled commitment to be a "Cheerleader for Manchester."The son of a town councilman from nearby West Haven, local politics is in Moran's blood. He has seen firsthand how local leaders can transcend prescribed political designations to serve a community. Decades ago, this was easier.

With both parties progressing towards their respective poles on the political spectrum and ideological disagreement destroying friendships, modern politics can be troubling. That said, there is great potential to heal some of these divides on the local level where Republicans, Democrats, and the politically inactive can disagree, while remaining connected. It's this connection that Mayor Moran aims to foster among Manchester's residents.

HOW MORAN IS EVERYONE'S CHEERLEADER

Moran is a self-identified "speech junkie." An avid listener to old, political speeches, he regularly embeds quotes in his own oration. While it's no surprise that Moran—a Democrat—integrates Obama and Clinton's words while addressing his community, he has also admitted to sometimes quoting Reagan. This is because, to Moran, good leadership is not a partisan issue. He cheerleads for *both* sides; to him, they're all part of the home team.In his leadership, Moran unwaveringly commits to prioritizing the people he has been elected to serve.

In this day and age, that's no easy task. Increasing polarization on the national level has divided all Americans, including the people of Manchester. As a moderate Democrat in the age of Trump, Moran has not only faced opposition from steadfast Republicans, but also from members of his own party."

When I chose a Republican as my Deputy Mayor," he explained, "many Democrats were mad at me." However, Moran stands by this move. In his view, the decision was attuned to his ultimate leadership goal: to bring his city's residents together. Every time election season rolls around, a wave of partisanship overwhelms the entire nation; Manchester is no exception. Formerly a large, predominantly white, middle class suburb, the town has expanded and diversified over recent decades. Though it leans leftwards today, a substantial Republican population makes for competitive elections. In Manchester, candidates for the Board of Directors don't campaign individually. Instead, each party runs a group of candidates and the top nine vote-getters win seats. This model inherently pits the two sides against one another, and understandably, sometimes things get heated.

According to Moran, while civility remains high among candidates, town committee members and local volunteers more often throw verbal punches. "I've seen nasty things about me on Facebook saying that I'm raising taxes or just attacking me for having a D next to my name," he explained. He has also been interrogated by voters in-person over local policy issues. Amidst the turbulence, Mayor Moran keeps his cool. He says that in these moments, you need to be, "thick skinned, quick on your feet, and honest, because you're better off saying you don't know the answer than lying."

Over his career, Mayor Moran has employed a mature, sensible approach to leadership; he aims to stand *above* partisan crossfire. After his election to the Board of Education, one of his colleagues turned to him and asked, "Do you really believe in this kumbaya?" Unlike many politicians, Jay Moran certainly does. He says, "We always have differences, but strong leaders realize they need to work with everyone." In his experience in local politics, "90% of the time, everyone's on the same page. Sometimes it takes a cup of coffee to straighten the differences out. Sometimes it just takes time."

WHY THIS APPROACH STRENGTHENS COMMUNITIES

Moran's style of leadership prioritizes community over politics. Politics is a major part of what he does, but it isn't the *only* part. "I can't go to the local supermarket or my church without people asking me questions," he says, adding that sometimes the produce aisle isn't his favorite place to take inquiries about the town's mill rate. That said, he understands that his position is inherently politicized and does accept that voter upset about budgets or building projects are part of the deal. Under his philosophy, this kind of communication, while potentially tense, is actually a good thing. For Moran, interacting with the town's many residents is a source of great fulfillment. To summarize his own experiences, he says, "You get into politics to make a difference, you stay because of the people you meet."

HOW COMMUNICATION HELPS

Harmonious equilibrium thus *can* be reached in local politics; one where groups, leaders and constituents work together to make decisions. Moran's strategies as mayor can only go so far if they are not met with a voter's willingness to engage. If these parties don't communicate, they can't benefit from one another. Good leaders are the ones who provide the opportunity for communication; good constituents are the ones who make the most of it.

Moran shared he was once confronted by a disgruntled Democrat, concerned at seeing the town's education budget cut. Though this resident heard about the budget slash, she didn't know that by law, the education budget couldn't be shrunk. Instead, it was only a proposed addition to the budget that was cut, and ultimately, funding for education ultimately rose. Left unacknowledged, this resident would have held onto a misconception that would have informed her view of the community and Moran. A single conversation with the mayor cleared it up.

Acknowledging that the local newspaper will fixate on conflict and controversy, Moran expressed frustration that positive moments just don't get covered. Few watched as Moran was hugged by a third grader thanking him for the park she plays in, or when Manchester's typically disengaged Bangladeshi community rallied in support after he visited their mosque. These are the moments that remind him why he went into politics in the first place.

WHY ANYONE CAN BENEFIT FROM DOING THIS

Politics doesn't require viewing the world in shades of red and blue, and the most important political moments don't take place behind the doors of City Hall. On a local level, people want to see—above all—personally engaging politicians who make it clear they care. That's why Jay Moran is willing to have a fruitful conversation with supporters and opponents alike, it's why Prasad Srinivasan committed hours of his life in public view on a street corner, and it's why we should gravitate towards, rather than away from, politics.

In my experience as a volunteer, I've gone to many places with candidates and officials within my community. Through this, I've learned political involvement can lead to increased community integration. One day, a pancake breakfast function taught me all about the Lions Club. By attending, I got to speak to the organization's leadership, hear about their mission, and inquire about membership. On another occasion, I attended a forum on potential affordable housing with some Glastonbury Town Councilmen and candidates. These instances took me outside of my echo chamber, taught me things I never expected to learn about, and introduced me to fellow community members along the way. I also got to see the way political figures interact with constituents (wearing a name tag and shaking hands). Instead of dismissing these figures as vote-grabbers, consider that locally, these people actually want to get to know you. They wouldn't be doing this otherwise.

They want to know us, so we should get to know them. They're our neighbors, and can be our friends too. Building these connections may even change how you feel about politics in general, or, better yet, get you excited.

CHAPTER 6:

THINKING OF IT AS AN EXTRACURRICULAR

———

"Local political involvement" is a broad term.

That's why so many things can constitute involvement. Paying more attention constitutes involvement; so does doing research before elections. Going to political meetings is another form of involvement, as is talking with a local candidate or elected official. All of these are available to voters who already engage in the political ecosystem. They're the ones marketed-to during campaigns, and they're the ones whose interests are represented by government officials. They're the ones who make up the majority of America.

Over the past few chapters, this group has been the target of our discussion. For them, taking small steps to increase awareness can grow into exponential involvement.

Then, there's another group: politicians, party officials, municipal board members, and local volunteers. They're the ones who put in the most time and energy to serve the public. They're the ones designing the campaign logos, building the platforms, preparing the talking points, and updating the social media pages behind the scenes.Because this book has already focused on similarities between political figures and the citizenry, its next goal is to highlight how citizens themselves can join this political group. It's far more possible than most realize, and the opportunities are endless.

I'll outline different ways local political action can be taken, but all rests upon the same foundation. Before getting involved, it's essential to understand how and why it's worth it. Yes, it does demand time and resources—but you get out as much as you put in.

HOW LOCAL POLITICS CAN KICKSTART A PROFESSIONAL CAREER

At the end of sophomore year of high school, a friend asked me, "What are you doing over the summer?" I answered like any fifteen-year-old would: sleeping in, going to the beach, wiping all memories of Algebra 2 from my brain.However, her reaction was baffled. "You're not working? Or volunteering? Or self-studying for another AP exam?" After spending a year barely scraping by in AP Biology, the last thing I wanted to think about was studying for another exam."Colleges don't want to see that you did nothing. Then you're at a disadvantage to everyone who did something" she explained, rattling my confidence in the future to the core. I did what any panicked teenager would've done amidst a dilemma in 2013: I posted on Yahoo! Answers. Within minutes, a slew of anonymous experts assured me that my college prospects would *not* be damaged by taking two months to enjoy being a kid. Though I enjoyed a summer free of responsibilities and homework, I learned firsthand that it's not just what you do in the classroom that matters, but also the things you do outside of it.

WHY IT CAN PRESUPPOSE ANY PROFESSION

After getting into college (yes, I *was* still able to), the pressure intensified. The goal was no longer to make oneself appear well-rounded in the eyes of an admissions officer— my peers were now even more concerned with resume bolstering experiences. Now, the game was sharpening professional qualifications in specific fields to eventually land a job. College students know that it's not just what you do in the classroom that matters, but also the things you take on outside. I didn't anticipate just how high the stakes would be during freshman year. I assumed I had a good three years before job-search fever and accompanying stress would sweep my social circle, but it came sooner than expected.

Once spring semester started, I saw everyone grappling with the question of summer internships. Lounging at the beach or mowing lawns have ceased to be enough of an experience for a young adult in this ultra-competitive world. Thus, an increased pressure to "make the most" of summer months.

Some classmates already had clear goals, and meticulously groomed their plans to reflect that. Aspiring doctors sought out hospital positions, aspiring lawyers looked toward firms. Some had narrower vision, singling out specific corporations to court (I'm looking at you, Big Tech), with the hopes of getting their foot in the door. This also manifested itself geographically: many temporarily uprooted themselves to distant cities for experience. Techies looked toward Silicon Valley, young financiers went to New York, and throngs of politicos flocked to Washington D.C.

However, not everyone has such a precise idea of their professional aspirations at such an early age. For those students, embarking on a rigorous internship application process and making a temporary move just doesn't seem worth it. Nearly a third of American college students change majors during their studies, with even fewer certain of a "dream job" throughout. These students don't know where to look, what to apply for, or how to start looking for summer rentals. They do, however, know that college is different from high school, and professional experiences do make a difference. I was one of these students, though what I did that summer should come as no surprise.

WHY IT'S A VIABLE OPTION FOR ANYONE

At eighteen, I was not ready to decide on a dream occupation, commit my soul to a certain company, or uproot myself to move cross-country. Part of me envied the Economics majors who, by February, had Wall Street internships lined up and leases signed, and proceeded with confidence down their early career path.

For me, I wanted to do something productive, fulfilling, and enjoyable. Because I lacked the crystal-clear future-vision some of my peers had, I knew I would rather advance my skill set in a generalized, rather than specialized, way. This would keep doors open without setting me back, giving me more time to figure out what to do. I returned home for the summer, knowing that I didn't need to be in a big city to do something worthwhile. Ultimately, I harnessed the political interest I'd been slowly but surely building and worked on a local campaign.

WHY THERE'S SO MUCH TO BE LEARNED

While it's all too easy to cling to prestige (desiring a company's clout or a fancy office for your Snapchat stories), it doesn't guarantee fruitful experiences. For young adults, the top priority should be to learn. There's a whole world out there beyond the classroom, and internship opportunities open the door. While interning on this particular campaign, what I did most was learn. Understandably, a lot of what I learned was political. I learned how to run a campaign, how a candidate communicates with voters, how messaging is spread, and how funds are raised, allocated, and spent. Simply by being present and observing, I was able to learn what happens behind the scenes of a local campaign.That said, most of what I learned wasn't campaign-specific at all. Since our team was small, I had my hands in a variety of tasks. My duties were so broad I essentially did whatever needed to be done. I learned how to speak properly on the phone and stay organized. I learned how to be a productive teammate and how to be indispensable to a superior. I learned how to network, conduct myself at formal events, and coordinate with others to make effective plans. Even though I did persist down this path, these general skills contributed to my maturation and would have served me well in any pursuit. I probably would not have learned so much about so many different things in such a short period of time, had I not worked on a local campaign.

HOW IT'S SO ACCESSIBLE

Because every inch of the States is represented politically, you don't need to travel far to play a part in politics. The scope is so wide, with so many positions, campaigns, and elections out there that supply is often higher than demand. While this contributes to unfilled positions, understaffed campaigns, and uncompetitive elections on the local level, it also means that ample opportunities exist for those who *do* want them.A "more the merrier" mentality exists where anyone with interest can be utilized. While it doesn't pay like the corporate world does, chances are you at least won't have to pay rent! Another notable advantage of working in local politics is weaker emphasis on a rigidly hierarchical structure like in other industries. Entrance is not limited to young applicants who then must compete against one another, funneling upward to leadership positions. While work experience is still crucial and advancement is still sought after, a wide array of political opportunities exist. If you meet the right people and are willing to work hard, landing a prominent role is absolutely possible.

Don't just take it from me—there are others who have found professional enrichment in local politics and benefited immensely because of it, like my acquaintance Ron Deb. After hearing what we've done, know that regardless of where you are, you could do it too.

HOW THERE'S SO MUCH ROOM FOR ADVANCEMENT

Ron was a former classmate, a year below me. We go way back, first meeting each other in Taekwondo as kids and continuing this extracurricular overlap in the high school Debate Club. Like most childhood connections, ours weakened after high school and we lost touch. Later on though— during one of my LinkedIn browsing sessions— Ron Deb's profile popped up. It read, "Connecticut's youngest campaign manager of 2018." This gave us a perfect reason to reconnect. Campaign manager is a substantial role, demanding significant time and sharp political acumen. Personally, I couldn't wrap my head around just how much it takes until serving as one myself.

I remember Catherine Marx—a veteran campaign manager and friend from Chapter 4—once conveyed just how extensive a campaign manager's duties are. "You need to inspire the candidate, you need to be artistic, you need to be managerial," she continued, "You're a coach, a messenger, a policy expert, a fundraiser, and a budgeter." If that's not enough, duties don't end when the workday is over—a campaign manager must always be, "watching a wide array of things: the candidate, the opposition, the party, and the national climate."This was Ron Deb's job. To make matters even more remarkable, he pulled it off while still enrolled as a college sophomore.

HOW RON GOT HERE

Though he advanced to such a prominent campaign role at nineteen, Ron recounted his trajectory with nonchalance. "After graduating high school in 2016, I was looking for something to do over the summer," he told me over a cup of coffee. His search led to State Senator Steve Cassano's reelection campaign (ironically, the candidate being challenged by Lorraine Marchetti, for whom I worked). Deb credits the Cassano campaign for providing him with a solid political foundation. While completing lower-tier tasks—such as making phone calls and fundraising—he was able to integrate himself within the campaign team. Cassano won reelection, and then, by 2018, it was campaign season again. Deb, upon finishing second year at the University of Connecticut, returned to the Cassano team to pursue a high-caliber position, taking on more substantial tasks. At this point, a Republican State Representative vacated his position to challenge Cassano, leaving a seat open for Democrats to vie for.

Jason Doucette, a 41-year-old lawyer and father, opted-in and needed a campaign manager. The Cassano team—deeply invested in their fellow Democrat's race—saw an opportunity for their bright, young staffer, and Ron Deb was up for the challenge.Stories like this are not uncommon in the campaign world. Opportunity is often a product of making connections, proving your competence, and being in the right place at the right time. In Ron's case, it was a perfect culmination of all of these factors that landed him this job. Though the scale was small, the scope of his responsibilities was huge.

As campaign manager, Ron's primary focus was on voter outreach and ground strategy during election leadup, since "Jason worked out most of his platform and policy ideas before I came on board." While Connecticut Democrats and political consultants outside of Hartford assisted with producing media and mailers, Ron's focus was overseeing day-to-day operations on-the-ground. He ensured that word of Doucette's candidacy and message swept across most houses in the 13th District.

HOW RON SPENT THESE MONTHS

Despite the heft of his job, upon reflection Deb coolly referred to the bulk of his duties as, "repetitive." This is because, over the six-month window, he spent substantial time sending out mailers, scheduling event appearances, and planning which neighborhoods to canvas on given days. One of his most mundane campaign experiences involved applying hundreds of small "President Barack Obama Endorsed Candidate" stickers to stacks of campaign literature. This proved to be an hours-long endeavor, which only Netflix could help him get through.

Deb's campaign duties also extended far beyond the secretarial. Though admin consumed his time on a daily basis, don't forget that campaign manager is a leadership role. Deb was *also* responsible for the challenging task of organizing and mobilizing volunteers (almost all of whom were significantly older). His role also came with the power to implement innovative ideas to guide the campaign towards success. This includes what he called the "Weekly Door Knocking Event." Each weekend, volunteers were invited to campaign headquarters to collectively cover targeted neighborhoods, while maintaining communal spirit. "We attracted more volunteers on the days that the big names came by," he reflected. These "big names" included Congressman John Larson and Senator Chris Murphy. Their appearances at these events attracted droves of volunteers looking to meet them, in addition to drawing attention to Doucette through photo opportunities alongside some of Connecticut's most prominent politicians.

WHY THIS IS UNIQUE TO LOCAL POLITICS

While volunteers are absolutely integral to the functioning of a healthy campaign, Deb did express some of the challenges associated with working above them. Aside from the obvious difficulty in attracting and retaining a solid volunteer base, coordinating volunteers once they are onboard can be an immense obstacle for campaign managers as well.

For example, the Doucette team was committed to adhering to a positive message, but one passionate volunteer had trouble suppressing anti-Republican rhetoric while knocking on doors. "I made sure he always went around with a buddy after finding out," says Deb. He also experienced similar difficulty on the sidewalk outside Glastonbury's 325th Birthday Celebration, where crowds of supporters held candidate signs. There, this same volunteer began shouting at a passerby sporting a "Make America Great Again" hat. Though the volunteer was a grown adult while Deb was a college student, it was his job to act the boss, stepping in to solve the problem. While a rarity in other industries, this kind of stuff can really happen in the world of local politics.

It may seem perplexing that a college sophomore was able to take all this on while continuing his studies. That's exactly how I felt hearing his story. School responsibilities consistently pulled me out of campaign mode just as they heated up, leaving me with only a few weekends to trek back home and help out.

Academic schedules can preclude many students from taking on substantial campaign roles, but Ron Deb leveraged it to his advantage. He found a way to register his campaign work as an "externship" through UConn's Political Science Department. While he continued to attend normal classes, he was also able to spend Tuesdays, Thursdays, and weekends as a campaign manager at home. Through receiving academic credit for this professional experience, he was able to take on this position, typically reserved for adults, as a student. Speaking retroactively about the race—Doucette defeated his opponent by a fifty-eight to forty-two margin, a defeat so substantial with a competitive seat even his team was surprised—I asked Ron if he felt his age worked to his advantage. He pondered for a moment, then nodded his head in affirmation. While he admitted to lacking experience and contacts, he described many of his day-to-day duties as, "learnable on the fly." He did credit his youth for helping with voters and party insiders, who, even if skeptical at first, were more often than not curious by the prospect of a nineteen-year-old in such a role. "I made sure to use my UConn email for everything. People liked seeing that," he says.

What's next for Ron Deb? Maybe Hartford. Maybe Washington, D.C. Maybe something outside of politics altogether.

Regardless, what he learned managing a local campaign will undoubtedly help him get there.

HOW ALL AGES CAN BENEFIT

Though these examples may suggest otherwise, the professional value derived from local political involvement is in no way limited to college students. Roles always exist that are open to anyone, anywhere, of any age. Only, of course, as long as you're willing to roll up your sleeves and get to work. Local political involvement—both on and off the campaign trail—is essentially a catch-all when it comes to professional experience. An incredibly wide array of skills and areas are represented in these operations. Teams require individuals with skill in sales, marketing, budgeting, graphic design, writing, scheduling, management, photography, event planning, and more. There is something up everyone's alley, and there's always the chance to strengthen other skills.

When I first attended a meeting of Glastonbury's Republican Town Committee (the local party chapter within my hometown), it was after graduating college. At this juncture, I was coming to terms with no longer being a student. For as long as I could remember, I had been defined by this particular characteristic. Now, there was no more classroom to return to. My involvement wasn't fleeting because I needed to pack up and leave over Labor Day weekend. Now I could see, from the perspective of an adult, what local political involvement looks like, and it was a lot more familiar than I anticipated.

WHY THIS IS A SATISFYING ADDITION TO LIFE

After parking at the community center, I entered the reserved room and picked up a printed agenda. The meeting began with the Pledge of Allegiance. Then we discussed matters like raising more money, sharpening social media presence, planning what to sell during an upcoming fall festival, and recruiting new members. The president was never mentioned, political issues never debated, voices never raised. To me, transitioning out of the academic bubble, it felt strikingly similar to extracurricular organizations I had been a part of over my school years. There's a chairman, a secretary, and a treasurer. There are events held and projects undertaken. Success depends on volunteer service.

Like with extracurriculars, participants have other things going on in their lives. They have families, and they have jobs. They're lawyers, doctors, business-owners, parents, and grandparents. Whether or not they ultimately seek office, they find enrichment through participating. Not only do they serve a cause within the community, they develop bonds with each other.On and off the campaign trail the same wide array of duties need filling, and there truly is something for everyone. If you're an accountant, there's always a need for a treasurer. If you're a restaurant-owner, there's always a need for event space. If you're tech savvy, there are always websites that need maintaining. If you own a truck, there are always signs and boxes that need transporting. For me, I know my way around a camera. This ability allowed me to find my own niche within the group.

HOW POLITICS DEPENDS ON PEOPLE TAKING ACTION

When people think about politics, the focus is often on words rather than actions. So many of our perceptions are shaped by policy positions, partisan disagreements, verbal attacks, and buzzword-laden slogans. For those who aren't particularly engaged, that's what is most visible. You hear them on television, you read about them in the newspaper, you cannot seem to avoid them on social media. A closer look, though, shows that it's so much more than that. Once you strip away the words and focus on what's behind them, you find *people*. It's people who design and distribute lawn signs you drive by on your way to work, and who left that campaign flyer on your porch. These people may be college students looking to amass professional skills, or they may be retirees who do it to remain active.

Regardless of how old you are or where you live, you can be one of these people. Investment of time and attention into local politics is crucial, and opportunities are plenty. Whether you're an eager youth looking to develop new skills or a fully-fledged adult looking to utilize existing experience, you can benefit from local politics. Between gaining literacy in the electoral process, amassing local connections left and right, and experiencing the fulfillment associated with investing yourself in your local community, it'll certainly be rewarding. The greatest reward arrives after spending a summer campaigning or volunteering on Election Day. It arrives when you see the fruits of your labor, after talking to constituents or composing an official campaign Facebook post yourself. That's when you realize you're not just benefiting from local politics, but local politics is benefiting from you.

CHAPTER 7:

FINDING MY COMMITTEE

———

Though you may understand why taking local action is valuable, it sounds pretty intimidating to hear "go do it!" If you're not a college student seeking temporary employment breaking into this world can sound difficult, especially if you don't know anyone. This shouldn't hold anyone back. Local politics is kept afloat by volunteers. These individuals, coming from various personal and professional backgrounds, join together in pursuit of a shared cause. Through this process bonds form, friendships grow, and teamwork solidifies. Because achieving this is easier said than done, I'll share my volunteer experience and how it intersected with the experience of one of my fellow volunteers.

HOW LOCAL VOLUNTEERING IS UNIQUE

I've learned one thing about politics: it's pretty damn addictive. As soon as you learn what's happening, you want to see it in action. As soon as you see it firsthand, you want to be a part of it. The pulse of our political system is dependent on people who choose to take this kind of action. In the national sense, taking voluntary action typically involves binding yourself to a candidate and their platform. When you attend a rally, you're volunteering your time to see and hear the candidate. When you contribute to a campaign, you're volunteering your money to support that cause. Even when you display a sticker, you're volunteering your bumper as advertising space.

This is the impression most people have of taking political action through volunteering. If you're willing to commit more, there are always doors that need knocking and phones that need calling. If you're willing to commit even more, larger-scale campaigns hire paid staffers who take on more responsibility.Even if it seems as though everyone around you is doing these things come general election season, looks can be deceiving. Despite all the individual donors Bernie Sanders touts or all the MAGA hats on display across the nation, most Americans don't volunteer often.

In 2016, eighty-one percent of Americans didn't attend a single rally for either a presidential or congressional candidate.

Eighty-five percent did not volunteer any of their time or money, and seventy-nine percent abstained from displaying a yard sign or bumper sticker.[22] Even if they did vote (and fortunately many of them did), driving to the polls was the only form of political action they took. While it's better than nothing, there's certainly room for growth. However, that particular discussion is only about political action on a national level. The focus of this book, on the other hand, is the local level: where district boundaries are mere miles away and candidates often reside within walking distance. While opportunities for action are similar (displaying signs, reaching voters, contributing funds), allegiances needn't be made to distant figures who may only visit your area as a once-off. With local political volunteering, you're supporting a local party and a local person.

HOW MY EXPERIENCE BEGAN

When I volunteered on Lorraine Marchetti's state senate campaign, I didn't know what to expect. However, there were a few things I *didn't* expect to do, and making friends was one of them. I was just an eighteen-year-old political enthusiast, volunteering to get some real-world experience.

---

22 Edwards-Levy, Ariel. 2016. "Volunteering For A Campaign Or Going To Rallies? You're In The Minority." Huffington Post. Accessed October 11 2019. https://www.huffpost.com/entry/campaign-volunteering-rallies-poll

In the earlier days of summer, things were going as planned. I either did my work alone or alongside Lorraine and corresponded directly with her. As the youngest person around, the campaign was my top (and only) priority, so I worked mornings and afternoons, sometimes from my own house and other times from hers.On my first day, I was given a hefty spreadsheet packet containing local voter name and phone numbers. I was confronted with every millennial's' most dreaded campaign task: calling, drumming up support, and asking for contact information. Unfortunately, this was 2016. Most people realized that offering up personal information to an inexperienced sounding cold-caller is not a wise idea, no matter how reputable they claim to be. I was met with a lot of rejection but am happy I got through it early on.

I also remember sitting alongside Lorraine at her kitchen table, sorting files and compiling folders of documents on her MacBook. This was doable work; plus, it plunged me into the nitty-gritty, acquainting me with mundane (albeit crucial) elements of campaign work. It also gave us a chance to personally connect, as our evaluation of spreadsheets and press releases eventually veered to reminiscing on old vacation photos. Still, though I knew others were involved with the campaign in some capacity I never saw any of them. For all I knew, we were a team of two: a candidate and her volunteer.

HOW IT CHANGED

Things changed after a few weeks after being invited to my first "campaign meeting." I wasn't sure what I was getting myself into because, unlike all of my other campaign obligations, this one took place in the evening. As I pulled up in front of the Marchetti household, I was greeted by an unfamiliar scene: the typically empty driveway was packed with cars. Once I entered the house, I was overwhelmed by the mass of new faces amicably conversing. I tried to stay out of the way. While everyone mingled, I stood in the corner snacking on chips and pretending to be engrossed by Don Jr's RNC speech playing on a nearby television. As the meeting started, I tried making myself useful, briskly carrying chairs over to the dining room. Concerned about there being enough space for everyone else to do their adult business, I lingered on the sidelines, surveying the room. That's when I heard Lorraine call, "Alex, get a seat for yourself!" I remember this as a legitimizing moment: to be offered a literal seat at the table. I thought I, if anything, deserved a corner seat. However, that wasn't the case. I went from viewing myself as a lowly college intern to an official team member.

Soon, I found that the dozen or so individuals on this team were volunteering because they were either a personal friend of Lorraine's (despite not being particularly politically active) or were involved with the local Republican

Party. In many cases, they were both. After years of shared service to a local organization and numerous campaigns, people bond. The reason I never saw them was because aside from volunteering their time to serve the campaign, they had jobs, families, and lives of their own.

HOW I BEFRIENDED MY TEAMMATE

As the meeting progressed, different duties were introduced and claimed. After a lengthy discussion on lawn signs (seems simple enough, but this stuff never is), the subject of capturing endorsements arose. A few volunteers were needed to coordinate and film video endorsements with prominent local figures. I, being the tech savvy stripling at the table, interjected that I could put my skills to use for filming and editing. I'd taken a videography class back in high school, so even though I was a little rusty, I knew my away around a camera.

This idea was met with enthusiasm from across the table, giving me a warm sense of belonging among strangers. I could sense a sigh of relief sweep over the table, because despite years of experience, media was still largely uncharted territory for many. Fortunately, there was a millennial who could bring something new to the table. Then, a woman sitting opposite me offered to help correspond with endorsers to schedule meeting times. She knew most of the people we'd be interviewing, so it was only natural that our skills would complement one another's.

WHY WORKING ALONGSIDE JUDY WAS SO SPECIAL

This woman was Judy Stearns, a retired kindergarten teacher, former elected official, and veteran political volunteer in Glastonbury. Over the ensuing weeks, we became a powerful duo, traveling across the district together, amassing endorsement footage. While I unfolded my tripod and unraveled my microphone's cord, she would converse with the interviewee. Then, while I filmed, she would ask questions like, "How do you know Lorraine?" and, "Why do you support her?"

Between interviews and during car rides, we had many opportunities to chat about both the professional and the personal. I learned about her sons and heard about her grandchildren. She also gave me excellent context about our interviewees. In fact, the first (and only) lightbulb I had ever changed was above her kitchen sink, after a busy day of filming. We weren't only teammates making video endorsements. Over those weeks, we developed an inter-generational friendship, between the team's freshest novice and longest serving member. We were bonded by our service to a shared political cause. Though we worked together to help Lorraine get elected, Judy and I rarely ever "talked politics." Instead, we "talked Glastonbury," commenting on the town's past, present, future, and the people living there. That's because—unlike national political volunteers—those on the local level have the strongest community allegiances. They're not always the most extreme or vocal. Instead, they are quietly passionate individuals who commit time and energy to strengthening their organizations and serving their communities. In doing so, they get to know each other very well.

HOW JUDY GOT HERE

Judy Stearns had made many friends through local politics. At each filming session, she seemed to already know each interviewee. We met with two State Representatives, a handful of board members, a few local party officials, and more. Judy started and finished each interaction by chatting about their families, jobs, and lives. At campaign meetings everyone on the team knew, respected, and appreciated Judy. Her deep integration into local politics was the product of decades of dedicated civic service to the town of Glastonbury, and I knew I was privileged to work alongside her.

Almost three years after the campaign had concluded, I met with Judy at our local Panera (a favorite meeting spot for local Republicans, for some reason). We'd once sat in the same booth to discuss the game plan for our endorsement project. This time, I asked what she had been up to since we last saw each other. "I helped out on Lillian's campaign doing mostly sign-waving on the corner," she recounted, referencing Glastonbury's candidate for State Representative in 2018, "and I was a planner of the Lincoln Day Dinner a few weeks ago," citing an annual Republican event. She then grieved that—due to a scheduling conflict with the Glastonbury Adult Chorus' rehearsal time—she hadn't been able to attend monthly meetings for Glastonbury's Republican Town Committee (GRTC).

WHY TOWN COMMITTEES ARE THE BACKBONE OF LOCAL POLITICS

I asked about what the Republican Town Committee actually *was*. I knew that most of Lorraine Marchetti's campaign team (in addition to most of our endorsement interviewees) were members of it. Over the years I had heard it (and the opposing GDTC) referenced, mainly during election season when both served as volunteer bases. Beyond that, I was completely in-the-dark on these organizations.

Recounting her experiences with GRTC, Judy explained that in addition to fundraising, event planning, campaigning, and volunteer recruitment, these organizations are responsible for selecting party nominees for municipal boards, town commissions, and legislative offices. Like most citizens, I've always learned which candidates are running a few months before election, when that information is publicly released. Intrigued by the seemingly immense political power held by these groups, I asked about membership and expected a lengthy application or competitive selection process. "You just need to go to a monthly meeting, which are open to everyone," she started with a smile, "and then, after your second, you are eligible to register as a member." I was shocked by the simplicity and ease. While I previously held a very campaign-centric notion of local, political involvement, joining a local party chapter is a way for individuals to engage without binding themselves to a single candidate. Plus, opportunities don't end on Election Day. Each state's party structures differ. While smaller states—like Connecticut, Massachusetts, and New Hampshire—divide local chapters by town bigger states, such as Iowa and Oregon, do so by county. Some states call them committees, some call them by other names. Regardless of where you are, volunteering with a local party chapter is an accessible way to get involved. There's always something to do, and anyone is welcome.

To me, it seemed similar to high school and college extracurriculars. As I shared in the last chapter, it ended up feeling that way too. Membership was voluntary, meetings were infrequent but regular, an executive board (chairman, vice chairman, secretary, treasurer) leads, and aside from taking on projects and holding events, it serves largely social purposes. I thought that if I ever moved to a new town, joining a town committee would be priority. With people to meet and important decisions to be made, I can't think of a better way to take political (and social) action!

HOW JUDY'S EXPERIENCE BEGAN

Judy's explanation had me ask about her own history with the GRTC. She said she first got involved with the local fifty years ago. As a young mother of three, new to the town of Glastonbury, she immediately began volunteering—just as her own mother had done in nearby West Hartford. Judy was exposed to local politics at a young age, and that sense of importance stayed with her into adulthood.

During the mid-century, men and women belonged to different organizations. Judy, as a result, served as a committed member of the Glastonbury Republican Women's Club. From her description, I got the impression that the group served as a valuable way to bring women together, while also getting things done. The children would play while Judy and the other women prepped mailers and conversed.

During the 1960's, women and men's groups integrated. Judy joined the newly unified Glastonbury Republican Town Committee, a group she stayed involved with for decades. During this lengthy tenure, she served on a number of municipal commissions—most notably, an eight-year stint as Vice Chairman and Majority Leader on the Town Council. She also chaired the Glastonbury Republican Town Committee twice, once in the 1980s and again in the 2010s. While raising children, maintaining a career, and involving herself with Connecticut's YMCA, Judy Stearns also consistently volunteered her time to local political causes, both on and off the campaign trail.

HOW TO VOLUNTEER OFF THE CAMPAIGN TRAIL

Years after working with Judy to record video endorsements, I received a call from George Norman, a Glastonbury Town Councilman from that initial campaign meeting back in 2016. It was early summer of 2019, before that year's municipal campaign season began and a year away from state legislative races. George was calling on behalf of the GRTC, to notify me of an upcoming project that was still in the brainstorming stage. At first, I was confused. I thought GRTC projects were either campaigns, or fundraisers for those campaigns. Once I found out what George had called about, I fell in love with the idea.

Glastonbury, like many other towns and cities, is run by a series of boards and commissions. While some—like the Town Council and Board of Education—get all the attention, others fly under-the-radar working behind-the-scenes to handle more specific aspects of governance. Glastonbury's website lists twenty-nine of these groups, ranging from the Water Pollution Control Authority to the Commission on Aging. All of these are run exclusively by volunteers. They may not be the ones waving in front of polling stations on Election Day, but they sit through grueling hours-long town meetings in addition to everything else they do.

This project's purpose was to meet with the chairs of these boards and commissions (most of them Republican) to shoot mini-documentary features on what they do. These clips would then be posted to our website and Facebook page.

My first shoot was with Barbara Theurkauf, who chairs Glastonbury's Historic District Commission. We sat at a picnic table outside of the Historical Society's meeting one morning and she explained to the camera that her commission was tasked with reviewing all proposed exterior house modifications on Glastonbury's historic Main Street. I've driven down this strip of Main Street every day I spend in town. Here, I'd pass exceptionally maintained homes, around for hundreds of years. Even so, I didn't know that in the 1980's, there was a push to tear many down and commercialize as much as possible. Barbara says that that's why the Historic District Commission was formed. After capturing some b-roll footage of the homes and editing together a five-minute video, she taught over 4,000 viewers the same thing. I learned a few important things during this project, both about my town and about political action. Most important was that local political volunteering doesn't begin and end with election season. Local party chapters operate year-round, and volunteerism isn't limited to campaigning. The GRTC continues to meet every month, even when the nearest election is barely in sight. Barbara Theurkauf will continue to devote significant time to preserving Main Street's charm, even if people admire its beauty without knowing the work behind it.

WHY ALL VOLUNTEERS DESERVE RECOGNITION

The purpose of this chapter is strikingly similar to that of GRTC's Boards and Commissions Project: to call attention to volunteers across America. The lack of recognition they receive is not only troubling because they deserve praise, but also because keeping them in the dark keeps people unaware or misinformed about nearby political action opportunities.

I urge you to look closer and discover volunteering for yourself. Even if skeptical about associating with one party or another, check both out to see where you feel a stronger sense of belonging. At its heart, politics is about people.

I cannot stress enough that local politics is vastly different from national politics. Conflating the two will only drive people away from the local. In my experience, national issues seldom come up at local gatherings. Instead, the focus is on municipal issues, community preservation, and one another. If it's not, there's a problem, and you're probably in the wrong place.

While politics may seem like the great polarizer, on a local level it can have immense unifying power. When I worked alongside Judy in filming endorsement videos, it didn't matter that we were at vastly different positions in our lives. It was my first campaign, while she had been involved with dozens. Nevertheless, we were able to team up behind a common goal, applying our individual skill sets to make an impact. Regardless of age, gender, or race, local politics is a way for service-oriented individuals to come together with the mutual of bettering the community. This is what members of both Republican and Democrat Town and County Committees do. It's what members of municipal boards and commissions do too.

It's what anyone can do.

CHAPTER 8:

RUNNING IN THE RIGHT DIRECTION

———

Stepping into the political world as a volunteer is simple, accessible, and flexible. After deeming local politics a worthy and rewarding cause, opportunities exist for all willing to commit their time and energy.

For some, though, this simply isn't enough. They deem the cause *so* worthy that they're willing to commit extensive time and energy to it—not simply as a side gig, but as a primary obligation. For these people, their action is significant and the challenge they face is daunting. No discussion of political action, after all, would be complete without mentioning running for office.

HOW TO SHAKE THE MISCONCEPTIONS

Many misconceptions exist about running for office, shaped largely by who we see doing so. It seems reserved for career politicians with decades in the game, or rich outsiders who can afford it by leveraging private sector connections and experiences. Forty is considered young, demographic diversification is still new, and everyone seems to have a law degree. Looking upwards at presidential candidates, senators, and governors, this still holds true in many cases. It's difficult to nab a top slot without working up the ladder or skipping a few rungs because you have the means. However, though these are the campaigns that garner widespread attention, there are also ones for lower positions. Making a run for governor is different from running for a seat in the State House, State Senate, City Council, or Board of Education. By lumping them all together, it's no surprise running seems inaccessible to average Americans. Since state and local legislative seats change hands infrequently, we assume that only established insiders have the access. However, if you have the motivation and guidance, running for local office is surprisingly accessible.

Age, race, and gender—all former barriers to office-holding— are ceasing to be such stringent limitations. According to the National Conference of State Legislatures, between 1971 and 2009, the percentage of women serving in state legislatures rose from four percent to twenty-five percent. The percentage of African-Americans rose from two to nine.[23] As of 2015 (when the most recent data was collected), the average age of state legislators in America was fifty-six, though ages ranged from nineteen to ninety-four.[24]

These statistics do not perfectly represent American public's demographic makeup: women comprise over half the country's population, African-Americans comprise thirteen percent, and the average age of American adults is forty-seven.[25] However, they *do* represent a major shift in the diversity of state and local leadership between the 1970s and 2000s. This has only intensified post-2010, with the most diverse slate of candidates emerging victorious in 2018.

Americans from all backgrounds are beginning to realize that running for office is more within reach than ever before. Though it's not an easy thing to do—physically and mentally—they're still going for it. And, they're actually winning.

WHY RUNNING IS MORE ACCESSIBLE THAN IT SEEMS

This is not a book about how to run for office (although I will mention some resources). It is, however, a book about

---

23 Kurts, Karl. 2015. "Who We Elect: The Demographics Of State Legislatures ". 2015. Ncsl.Org. Accessed October 11 2019. http://www.ncsl.org/research/about-state-legislatures/who-we-elect.aspx.

24 Ibid.

25 Ibid.

cultivating and acting on political impulse. I've stressed already that doing so is accessible, flexible, and both personally and socially fulfilling. Running for office sits at the peak of all the different ways to get involved. It entails sacrificing your privacy and opening up yourself to scrutiny, devoting exhausting hours to campaigning, and taking risks for an unsure outcome. However, it also entails being face-to-face with your neighbors, developing literacy of community issues, and, if successful, affording the power to exercise beliefs as a leader.It doesn't matter who you are or where you come from. All of this is possible when you set your sights locally. There is no town, county, or state in America without political representation. Though many of these seats are overlooked by the public, met with complacency from some established officials, and cyclically controlled by the same party, it doesn't have to stay this way. It can all be changed by motivated, enthusiastic, hard-working Americans who recognize that running for office is doable.

HOW ART LINARES DID IT

This is what happened in 2012, within Connecticut's Thirty-third Senate District. Comprised of ten small towns in the southern Connecticut River Valley, the quiet district had been represented by the same popular Democrat for two decades. When word got out that this incumbent wouldn't seek reelection, Democrats wanted to keep it and a Green Party challenger emerged.

Then, there were the Republicans. The district was rural—giving them somewhat of an advantage. Plus, the Green Party candidate might split the Democrat vote in their favor. As this unfolded, Art Linares was graduating college. With a degree in entrepreneurship from the University of Tampa, Linares returned to his Thirty-third District hometown Westbrook, Connecticut. His intention was to work for a commercial renewable energy company he co-founded. However, Linares' interests were not limited to business. At twenty-three, he was also incredibly politically-minded.A few years prior, Linares interned at Florida Senator Marco Rubio's Washington, D.C. office. Here, he got to see the inner workings of federal government, up-close. Linares shared, "While I was in Washington, I heard from a very successful government official that if you want to be an elected official, you just have to put your name on the ballot." Basically, Linares was told that running for office was doable if he was willing to put himself on the ballot. That's what Marco Rubio did in 1999, when he successfully ran for a Florida Legislature seat at age twenty-eight. This advice was fresh in Linares' mind when he returned home after college and discovered an open State Senate seat. Like Rubio, Linares was Cuban-American, Republican, and willing to put his name on the ballot at a young age.

Linares knew the road would be challenging. He was twenty-three, fresh out of college, and a complete newcomer. He didn't fit the typical mold of State Senate candidate—especially next to his Democrat opponent, a middle-aged State Representative who'd previously been a Selectman. Art Linares was confident and energized when daunted as a fresh face. His outlook and demographic played a major role in the trajectory of his campaign. "My age was a disadvantage prior to getting the nomination," he recalled, "but it was an enormous advantage during the general election.

"Linares' major pre-election obstacle was breaking into the ranks of an established party structure. It is party delegates from towns who ultimately select their candidate. Linares first needed to meet and court them, in order to clinch an endorsement. Prior to the party's convention, the nomination he sought was contested, with another potential Republican candidate in the mix; he needed to personally and persuasively rally candidacy support among municipal Republican party delegates, who flat-out did not yet know him. He cited this as a major difficulty for political neophytes, since, "Delegates are not people who vote the same way the electorate does." These delegates have usually been around for a while, and are endowed with significant deciding power in awarding nominations. Though they ultimately vote at an official convention, Linares explained that personal connections and relationships are regularly prioritized over ideas, message, or overall electability. Since he couldn't change these systems, Linares knew that he needed to cultivate those delegate relationships to stand a chance.

It wasn't easy—but his enthusiasm and motivation compensated for lack of pre-existing connections.

Ultimately, he won the nomination through working hard and smart. "First of all, I called every single delegate. Anyone who would talk to me, I tried to win over on the phone. If they wouldn't talk on the phone, I tried to set up a meeting with them personally," he explained. He eventually even resorted to showing up on the doorsteps of delegates he couldn't reach.

He also built relationships with community party leaders, since delegates often look to them for guidance. With every local party chapter equipped with its own leadership and volunteer base, decades of experience and advice can be tapped into by developing relationships here. These people have been in the game for years, and already they know all the things that new candidates need to learn.

HOW AGE WAS ACTUALLY AN ADVANTAGE

Youthful enthusiasm and dedicated motivation continued to serve Linares, well into the election. When he no longer needed to show up at delegate doors, he started visiting thousands of voters within his district to meet as many people as possible. During his campaign, Linares personally knocked on 10,000 doors, ensuring face-to-face time with an incredible number of voters. In a rural district with hilly, winding roads, covering that much ground was no easy feat.

Linares actually wore three pairs of shoes down to their soles. "Our first mailer was actually a picture of my shoes," he said, smiling. When they were no longer wearable, he hung them up at the entrance of campaign headquarters, a symbol of his dedication to connect with voters. A staunch supporter of the door-knocking strategy, Linares even made the claim that it's the only way to win. "It leaves a serious impression and shows that you work hard," which voters found extremely refreshing coming from a confident newcomer. It's also something any candidate can do, regardless of experience, money, or party. As long as you have the time (and shoes) to spare, personal outreach can be done simply and effectively.

Both before and after Linares' nomination, he prioritized personal connection to make a big impression. He didn't have incumbent status or decades of relevant experience on his side. Frankly, those things are not prerequisites for making a successful run. Newcomers with an appetite for action can accomplish great things by putting in the work and having fun with it. This is how, in 2012, Art Linares became Connecticut's youngest state senator at twenty-four.

HOW HE WAS SUPPORTED

Campaigns never won alone, and Art Linares' victory was no different. With so many roles, tasks, and duties, even the hardest working candidates need help. Amassing a team may sound difficult for a political newcomer who can't afford staffers and doesn't have interns lining up to help, but even the greenest novices needn't look too far for support.Despite enthusiastically accomplishing a lot by working hard himself, Linares is quick to credit those around him who helped along the way. On his campaign, these were family members.He gave campaign manager to his brother, who combined his organizational acumen with his deep understanding of his brother to ensure a smooth campaign. Linares recounted that, "Every day, he would tell me what I had to do, what neighborhood I had to cover." This allowed for Linares to shift focus towards covering ground and maintaining public presence. Linares was lucky to have someone so close to him take on such a critical role. In reality, most of us also have close contacts that can be counted on for help. If it's not a sibling, it can a best friend, parent, or neighbor. While political experts possess well-developed instincts, connections, and ideas, not every candidate has access to them or the money to hire one. Fortunately, a lot can be learned on-the-fly, so you may be surprised who'll make themselves helpful.

Aside from campaign managers, teams need eager volunteers who can maintain a solid presence on-the-ground: doors, street corners, events, or polls. The more bodies there are, the more noticeable the campaign, so there is great advantage in a coalition to get your name out. Once again, Linares called upon his family to assist.

Coming from a big, close-knit family, Linares expressed how blessed he was to have so many cousins working beside him as a task force. He noted that on Election Day, all of his family members took the day off to cover each of the district's polling stations. While there, they handed out small wafer cards (appropriately nicknamed "Magic Wafers") to voters on their way into the precinct. These wafers read "Art Linares for State Senator," with some encouragement to, "Vote for my Cousin/Brother/Son"—yet another signature personal touch from the Linares campaign.

It's easy to feel discouraged by the prospect of running for office. That said, the power of the newcomer shouldn't be underestimated on the campaign trail. Someone who has been through multiple campaigns may be complacent, while someone who *hasn't* might go above-and-beyond, trying to do things right. Someone who's been on the scene for years may make face-to-face contact a lower priority, while someone who hasn't can approach myriad voters, eager to make an introduction. A veteran may have established connections, but *anyone* can have passionate supporters willing to assist and vouch for them along the way.

Even if it doesn't seem so, the door to running for local office is always open. If you are willing to put in the effort, there's no reason not to walk through it.

HOW TO BEGIN

Running for office may sound easier said than done, especially coming from me (someone who has been around candidates and campaigns enough over the years to have a direct idea of what's involved). Plus, in Art Linares' case—though he was young—he had longstanding political interests that guided him to Rubio's office and then on to the ballot, giving him somewhat of an advantage.

This doesn't mean that a total novice's move-making is out of the question. Sure, if you've never volunteered on a campaign, attended a chapter meeting, or acquainted yourself with community issues and figures, you *will* be at a disadvantage. For anyone remotely considering making a run, these are the best and easiest places to start—they'll help you decide if this is something you truly want to do.

Even with this foundation, the intimidation of going forward can be a deterrent for many, especially those who feel like they're jumping in alone. Fortunately, this problem has been recognized as something driving fresh faces away and keeps office-holding feel out of reach. Especially in light of recent technological advancements, we are more connected than ever—allowing for instruction and support to be given, even from afar.

WHY CAMPAIGNS AREN'T WON ALONE

In the lead-up to the 2018 midterms, when Democrats (successfully) ran an unprecedentedly diverse group of candidates in state and local elections across the country, many political newcomers realized how accessible being elected could be. Again, the energy and drive that generally accompanies a fresh candidate does wonders in building a constituent relationships. We all saw Alexandria Ocasio-Cortez win in a major upset against Congressman Joe Crowley, a ten-term incumbent—largely by hitting the streets of the Bronx and demonstrating directly to voters that she culturally, racially, and financially related to them better than their current rep.

Again, though, campaigns are not won by this alone. Ocasio-Cortez had some help backstage—most notably from Bernie Sanders—but hundreds of victors in lower-profile races didn't have that privilege. Nevertheless, there are still hands for neophytes to hold as they embark into the political sphere.

HOW TO FIND THIS SUPPORT SYSTEM

It was a few months before Election Day; an article popped up on my Facebook feed about Will Haskell. Since this was clearly a political article shared by a Connecticut news source, it comes as no surprise that I went ahead and read it. It outlined the story of a 2020 candidate, sounding oddly familiar. Right out of college, the former congressional intern moved back to his home state Connecticut in pursuit of a seat in the State Senate. A Democrat who attended Georgetown, Haskell's strategy was to capitalize on his accessibility, relatability, enthusiasm, and social media mastery. Just like Ocasio-Cortez, Haskell successfully defeated an established incumbent.As I dug deeper into research, as I do whenever a new political figure appears on my radar (and as everyone should do after reading this book), I saw his biography on an interesting website: runforsomething. net. Here, I discovered that the organization—Run for Something—was a modern innovation that existed solely to help new candidates, well, run for something.

I learned a great deal about this organization through learning about its founder, whose backstory was not too different from mine. Amanda Litman is the epitome of a politico: a Washington, D.C. native whose interest was sparked by the West Wing, first got involved with local politics, and then ultimately worked on Barack Obama's presidential re-election campaign after graduating college.From there, Litman spent a lot of time at the top of the political food chain, working as a staffer on high profile campaigns. After a stint as Charlie Crist's digital director in an unsuccessful 2014 Florida gubernatorial bid, Litman reemerged into the world of presidential politics as email director on Hillary Clinton's 2016 campaign. Litman recounted the exhaustion of working on such campaigns, where, "You were there from 8:00 a.m. until 2:00 a.m. every night. We worked in the office seven days a week."[26] However, by the same token, she loved it, was willing to commit to it, and kept coming back for more.

Then, the results came in. Hillary Clinton's surprising defeat by Donald Trump sent shockwaves across the nation. While some celebrated the insurgent plunge of a political outsider into executive office, others were dismayed and

---

26 "Episode 18: Amanda Litman '12 On Her Passion For Progressive Politics". 2019. Alumni.Northwestern.Edu. Accessed October 11 2019. https://www.alumni.northwestern.edu/s/1479/02-naa/16/interior.aspx?pgid=28858&gid=2&cid=50056.

fearful. Understandably, Litman belonged to the latter group. However, she also recognized that there were many others across the country who felt the same way, though without her political knack and impressive experiences.Instead of using this loss as motivation to enhance her own political resume, Amanda Litman shifted her focus from the single highest office in American government to all the lower ones across the nation.

HOW IT CAME TO BE

As a political insider, Litman found herself repeatedly asked for advice from friends considering runs for office in the fallout of the 2016 election. Predominantly liberal millennials who'd never considered public office, these fresh aspirants were galvanized by Trump's victory. Realizing the best way to remedy their political discontent was with action, they needed to know how to make it happen.

Representing the fundamentally American ideal that anyone can run for office—regardless of qualifications (or lack thereof)—many took note of Donald Trump's outsider win as testament for what's possible in politics. Unfortunately, these mobilized individuals lacked the means and clout to forcefully plunge into the political realm like Trump. That's where Amanda Litman came in, using insider expertise to open up the possibility of local officeholding to gung-ho progressives across the country.realizing that, "at the time there wasn't an organization that existed that if you were young, and you were really excited about politics, and wanted to do more than just vote or volunteer," she took action, starting an organization called Run for Something, alongside another campaign veteran named Ross Morales Rocketto.[27]

On Inauguration Day 2017, Run for Something launched. Its mission statement is:*"Run for Something will help recruit and support young diverse progressives to run for down-ballot races in order to build a bench for the future... We aim to lower the barriers to entry for these candidates by helping them with seed money, organization building, and access to trainings needed to be successful."*[28]

Its initial goal was to recruit one hundred local office-seekers across the country. In the first week, 1,000 signed up. Since then, Run for Something has helped over two hundred candidates win local elections in forty states, with resounding success during the 2018 midterms. Of these victors, "55% are women and 50% are people of color."[29] From ultimate novices securing positions on municipal boards to legislative seats, Run for Something's commitment to progressivism brought

---

27   Ibid.
28   "Our 2019–2020 Strategic Plan". 2019. Medium. Accessed October 11 2019. https://medium.com/@runforsomething/run-for-somethings-2019-2020-strategic-plan-a272e5633849.
29   Ibid.

change to the most neglected corners of U.S. government. In doing so, "The number of uncontested elections on the state legislative level went down – from 40% in 2016 to 33% in 2018," not only advancing their cause but also revitalizing democracy in places where it had stagnated.[30]

Through raising money from progressive donors and building substantial volunteer networks, Run for Something provides both instruction and support to its myriad candidates. This involves screening applicants to ensure their commitment and authenticity, providing instruction on running a campaign, and cultivating a network of candidates and volunteers who share a desire for political change.

The work that Litman does for Run for Something is quite the departure from her tenure on presidential campaigns. She's fully gone local, cheerfully describing her new gig as "the best job in politics by a landslide."[31]

WHY IT WAS SUCCESSFUL

Run for Something should be seen as a political innovation unique to the modern era. The organization has had a major hand in making services more accessible in ways not previously

---

30 Ibid.
31 *"Episode 18: Amanda Litman '12 On Her Passion For Progressive Politics"*.

possible. Following the 2016 election, throngs of diverse individuals increasingly considered the prospect of public service but didn't know how to do so. Litman's organization was able to capitalize on this growing need and expedite the process—using expert insight to open previously locked doors.

21st Century technological advances, of course, have been crucial to Run for Something's resounding success. Previously, there was no way for seamless and direct communication among individuals across the entire country. Through harnessing the power of tools such as, "Trello, Slack, Google docs, ActionNetwork, ActBlue, and Zapier," to make information exchange easy, local campaign teams don't have to go it alone.[32] This allows for Litman's team of experts to assist and teach a new generation of politicians without the barriers once in place. They'll provide answers to questions such as, "how do I run Facebook ads? Or what should I say on my stump speech? Or how do I figure out what voters to talk to?" which are usually only known after years spent in the industry.[33]

HOW TO SEEK ASSISTANCE IN OTHER FORMS

Litman's project is indicative of the changing paradigm this book centers on: refocusing our political attentions onto

---

32 *"Our 2019–2020 Strategic Plan"*.

33 *"Episode 18: Amanda Litman '12 On Her Passion For Progressive Politics"*.

lesser elections that typically go unnoticed. Run for Something is one, well-developed organization that specifically backs progressive candidates. Though it assists only individuals with this particular alignment, its core theme is not at all partisan.

It's designed to open doors for dedicated individuals with a desire to pursue elected office. The candidates put in the on-the-ground effort, the organization provides expert instruction to ensure they're not completely alone in doing so.While I've yet to find a resource as cohesive and all-encompassing as Run for Something, there are other ways fresh candidates can receive support and instruction while campaigning. Recently, I saw a posting from the Connecticut Association of Boards of Education listing four workshops from across the state titled "So You Want to Be a Board Member? A Briefing on Preparing for Public Office." In-person classes like this *do* exist, and with the internet, candidates can easily search for local opportunities to learn more.

The internet also opens up a delightful Pandora's Box of blog postings, articles, and videos covering a wide array of topics. One of my personal favorites is political consultant Jay Townsend's YouTube, whose repertoire includes videos such as "What You Must Tell Voters First in a Political Campaign" and "Your Story: Your Secret Weapon in a Political Campaign."

Obviously, personalized guidance is immensely helpful, and political consultants for hire do exist. However, they don't come cheap, which causes campaign inaccessibility. Fortunately, there are other political consultants out there, not looking to be hired: elected officials, former candidates, town committee members, and habitual volunteers who know the ins-and-outs from years of experience. They reside in every community and are committed to political action. They also understand the specific characteristics of the community that every candidate must keep in mind. Are lawn signs frowned upon? Are local newspaper ads effective? Who are the best people to know or donors to reach out to? Questions like this cannot be effectively answered by a removed organization that provides more general support.

Communities are unique, so it's understandable that their politics are as well. That's why, if you're truly interested in running for office, get to know some of these local insiders. Talk to them, volunteer for them, and learn from their stories.

CHAPTER 9:

MAKING MEDIA
THAT MATTERS

———

A lot of things have changed for me between 2008 and 2019. I now know how to cook, I can say I've tried out having facial hair, and I've spent hours volunteering in local politics. A few things, on the other hand, haven't changed. My bedroom hasn't been redecorated, my height is still painfully average, and my enthusiasm shoots through the roof as soon as presidential election season rolls around.

Though I watch things unfold with more mature eyes and know lower ticket races are more relevant and accessible to me, the circus is still worth following. The iconic personalities involved, the constant coverage it receives, and the universal attention it commands make it arguably the biggest shared experience Americans are subject to. Do I now recognize it's not the be-all-end-all? Yes. Have I stopped trying to start debates about it every chance I get? Yes.

Has the way I follow the presidential election changed at all over the years? Yes, it certainly has.

HOW TIMES HAVE CHANGED

There has been one profound change distinguishing 2008, 2012, 2016, and 2020 for me. During the former two, I got my fix sitting eagerly in front of the TV, turning the volume up when new stations talked about the election and changing to another station as soon as they stopped. Not only was this pretty inefficient, the discourse was always driven by commentators opining on matters and arguing when they disagreed. Clips of candidates were often shown, but most of the time was spent talking *about* them. This was normal, I liked it, and I emulated it in my own life. Fast forward to 2016—print and broadcast media were officially joined by powerhouse social media. Before the 2016 presidential election, thirty-five percent of people between eighteen and twenty-nine reported social media as "the most helpful source of [election] information."[34]

---

34 Kapko, Matt. 2016. "How Social Media Is Shaping The 2016 Presidential Election". CIOcio. Accessed October 11 2019. https://www.cio.com/article/3125120/how-social-media-is-shaping-the-2016-presidential-election.html.

Social media's hold on presidential politics has only strengthened since its full roll-out in 2016. Iconic Trump tweets, Hillary logos overlaid on thousands of profile pictures, and the Facebook-Cambridge Analytica scandal will all be memorialized as symbols of social media's powerful political debut.

HOW THESE TRENDS FUNNEL DOWNWARDS

I wasn't merely a political spectator in 2016, only *receiving* social media programming. I was working on a campaign (if you haven't heard yet) and using my social media acumen to the campaign's advantage. I spent the entire summer carrying my camera with me everywhere I went to capture campaign images for social media. After a while, it began to feel like an appendage. My campaign cameraman philosophy was to capture as much as possible. Every public appearance posed a new challenge: too dark or bright, too busy or sparsely attended, etc. While Lorraine mingled with voters, I hovered behind, getting different angles, conversations, and expressions without being (too) overbearing. Not only did this allow us to compile an arsenal of shots, it also documented our visits on social media. Looking at an artist's handmade greeting cards—captured. Chatting with our congressional candidate—captured. Chowing down on a bowl of shortcake—also captured.

The power of self-coverage is an innovation all campaigns reap the benefits of, but its value is greatest for local campaigns. While a presidential candidate's event appearance is usually met with press coverage, local candidates and officials don't typically have that luxury. Facebook and Instagram posts can easily make a politician's appearances more visible and transparent, accessible even to those not physically in attendance. Local political figures' unfortunate lack of popularity can make them largely unknown or unrecognizable to voters. There's no better indicator of someone's prominence than paparazzi—it'll undoubtedly make people notice that someone important is present. Chances are, they'll wonder who it is.

The best part is, all that's needed for this are free social media accounts, a quality camera, and a dedicated amateur photographer.

HOW VIDEO BREATHED NEW LIFE INTO LOCAL POLITICS

Though a picture is worth a thousand words, in the campaign world a video is worth even more. Not only can video provide more immersive viewing experiences—drawing viewers in with visuals and sounds—it's also able to more directly convey information, using audio rather than displaying text.

From the mid-twentieth century to now, video has been an extremely popular and effective mechanism for campaign advertising. Candidates running for president, congress, and various statewide offices have consistently purchased television commercial space preceding Election Day, in an effort to grab wide attention and convey a message. This message can be positive, like Reagan's iconic "Morning in America" from 1984 that highlighting his success during reelection with statements such as, "Today, more Americans will go to work than ever before in our history [...], under the leadership of President Reagan, our country is prouder, and stronger, and better."[35]

An ad's message can also be negative, aimed to weaken the standing of a candidate's opponent. These kinds of "attack ads" can also be extremely powerful, like Johnson's 1946 "Daisy" ad which depicts a nuclear explosion, followed by narrative warning viewers to vote for President Johnson over his dangerous opponent—Barry Goldwater—because, "the stakes are too high for you to stay home."[36]

While these noteworthy ads have survived over time and have been credited for influencing election outcomes, thousands

35 Mark Joyella. 2016. "10 Iconic Presidential Campaign Ads That Changed Political Advertising". Adweek.Com. Accessed October 11 2019. https://www.adweek.com/tv-video/10-iconic-presidential-campaign-ads-changed-political-advertising-172600/.

36 Ibid.

of political videos are produced cycle after cycle. While television ads still remain prominent due to their unavoidable nature and wide-reaching audiences, they have dwindled into the 2010s.

While in 2012, almost fifty-eight percent of U.S. political ad dollar allocations went towards broadcast television, that percentage dropped to less than forty-five in 2016. Over the same period, spending on digital ads jumped from less than two percent to over fourteen percent. [37]

As we spend less time watching broadcast television and more time on the internet, substantial changes in campaign advertising funds allocation make sense. It's also critical to note, however, that advertising these two mediums does not come at the same cost. Television advertising is far more expensive than social media—both in production and distribution.

Television ads are generally limited to around thirty seconds. They also must be television-quality, meaning they need professional crews. For most campaigns, there are only so many times they can assume these expenses, so they're

37 David Erickson. 2017. "US Political Ad Spend Allocations – 2016 Vs 2012 [CHART] – E-Strategy Trends". E-Strategy Marketing Trends. Accessed October 11 2019. http://trends.e-strategyblog.com/2017/06/14/us-political-ad-spending-allocations-2012-vs-2016/28442?fbclid=IwARorjgKE86q7kEjBx9EMpkfBxENHDolDSu7y6RjAEOgaNIpngvA9kjKRFbA.

limited in what can be showcased on TV. There are also more restrictions to airing the ad. Charging at least a few hundred (but often a few thousand) dollars to air, popular stations can air ads state or nationwide. For a presidential campaign, with wider-reach and a bigger budget, advertising nationally makes sense. However, the prior restrictions can be unduly burdensome to smaller campaigns. In 2018, a hard-fought primary race in Connecticut's 5th Congressional District utilized the power of television. Both candidates put out commercials on broadcast television stations, and viewers saw them aired dozens of times. While this may sound like an effective strategy, thousands of people who saw the ads (myself included) didn't even live within the 5th District. Our views were costing the candidates money, but our votes couldn't help them in the slightest.

WHY THIS IS GOOD NEWS FOR LOCAL CANDIDATES

Fortunately, a more accessible option exists in the age of social media. DIY campaign ads—of any length, which need not be of professional quality—can be posted on social media and "boosted" to viewers. Anyone with Facebook knows how easy it is to take a moment to watch a video while scrolling down your news feed. Though most "Tasty" videos probably pop up because you like the page or one of your friends does, boosting a video awards it the same real estate, for a slight fee. Furthermore, specific zip codes can be targeted, ensuring that only people within a specified district see it. I was initially skeptical of this method. In a lot of ways, it seemed too good to be true. That was until I saw the big difference a little advertising can make.

HOW THIS CAN REVOLUTIONIZE CAMPAIGN ADVERTISING

Municipal elections are notoriously difficult. They don't coincide with big ticket races and—unless there's a heated race—there are usually too many candidates for councils and boards for voters to easily keep track of. Thus, not a lot of general awareness. When the Glastonbury Republicans launched their slate of candidates for the 2019 election, they posted a list of names and a group photo on their Facebook page. This reached 381 people organically, meaning most viewers liked the page already and likely didn't need swaying.

A few weeks later, a campaign kickoff event was held where guests were encouraged to meet the candidates. Knowing these candidates needed a chance to introduce themselves to voters who weren't at the event, I pulled aside the five Town Council candidates and three Board of Education candidates. In front of the camera, they all introduced themselves (something that only took ten seconds) before getting a group clip of them chanting "Vote Republican!" in unison. Afterwards, I compiled these introductions, spliced in some shots of event attendees, set it to upbeat music, and concluded with the candidates' message to "Vote Republican." After an hour or so of editing, the video was posted to Facebook and another team member boosted it. Within a few days, we had reached 1,236 Glastonbury residents, all for just ten dollars.

HOW FOLLOWING CANDIDATES NO LONGER REQUIRES ANY TRAVEL

When video is used well, it can do wonders for a campaign of any size. It affords candidates the freedom to show and express whatever they please; they can provide viewers an enjoyable experience that doesn't even need to feel like a commercial.

Take Tulsi Gabbard, the Hawaii Congresswoman running for president in 2020, for example. Though she never attracted much media attention, she used video to maintain an impressive web presence to clearly display her and her platform. The fact that she's married to a cinematographer helps. Tulsi Gabbard's Facebook page contains many traditional elements of a modern campaign. There are news articles supporting her platform, Facebook live videos where she speaks directly to viewers, regular updates on how many donors have contributed, and graphics branded with her campaign logo showcasing her notable quotes.

However, in a race where in-person appearances are geographically challenging and mass-media coverage is glutted by other candidates, Gabbard and her husband—Abraham Williams—found a solution, and they called it TulsiTV. As Gabbard has embarked on her nationwide campaign tour, she has been followed by Williams and his video camera. As she carries out typical candidate duties on the road (engaging with voters, making appearances at events, and selling herself), he records it all in ultra-high definition. Then, the clips are edited into short episodes incorporating shots of the scenery, Gabbard sharing her vision, and voters telling their stories. Then comes upload to Facebook, Instagram, and YouTube.

This tactic has been adopted by other candidates: Joe Biden, Amy Klobuchar, and Pete Buttigieg. All of these campaigns and more have uploaded video coverage of events to Facebook and Instagram. These typically comprise a few scenes of the candidate speaking, the crowd listening, and crowd interaction. This type of video provides insight into the event, bringing it to life.Gabbard's videos are more interesting, in my opinion. Averaging a few minutes long, they aren't advertisements in the conventional sense. They feel more like video exposés showing Gabbard firsthand—even if watching from thousands of miles away—not just from the perspective of an event attendee, but as an insider with access to her thoughts.

HOW TULSI'S VIDEOS CAST POLITICS
IN A DIFFERENT LIGHT

In her third video episode, Gabbard travels to Laconia, New Hampshire to meet with local leaders and town residents. After establishing scenes of the campaign team traveling by car through the bucolic, snow-blanked streets, we see Gabbard seated at a dining room table, in a recovery home for men dealing with substance abuse. Rather than documenting Gabbard selling herself to the group, the episode gives the viewer a seat at the table. For most of the segment, the focus is on the men, rather than the candidate, as they share their personal stories of addiction and recovery.

Only later does the attention pivot to Gabbard, who responds to the men rather than the camera. "Getting to the root cause of the problem, this is central to what we're talking about, but when you look at so many of the other challenges we face, often the answer is a reaction and it's a superficial one," she explains, tying the meeting back to her platform in a way that's satisfying to both those in-person and those watching online.[38]

In another episode, Gabbard is shown on a civil rights pilgrimage through Alabama. She goes to the Liberty Museum in Montgomery, studying monuments and statues that

---

38 "Tulsi TV – On The Road – Episode 3: Laconia, Plymouth". 2019. Youtube. Accessed October 11 2019. https://www.youtube.com/watch?v=iwjclSoI9UU.

recognize the region's painful history of slavery and discrimination. Then, she is shown crossing the iconic Edmund Pettus Bridge in Selma, days before the anniversary of "Bloody Sunday," on which law enforcement officers brutally attacked a group of unarmed marching activists in 1965. Though Gabbard is visible in most of these scenes, she stands respectfully towards the back of a crowd of commemorators. As the scenes roll, the crowd's soulful rendition of "This Little Light of Mine" plays. Though this somber occasion was not an opportunity for stump speeches or courting voters, the way it was captured on video made it suitable for campaign purposes. She closes with the message, "There is more work to be done."[39]

With no patriotic background music or flashy graphics in sight, these episodes are hypnotically immersive, as if we're on the campaign trail alongside her. There's no better medium than video to convey the essence of a candidate to those without the luxury of firsthand experience.

HOW THIS CAN BE REPLICATED ON A SMALLER SCALE

Videos are not necessarily advertisements or commercials, and the fact that social media allows for a wider variety of

---

39 "Tulsi Gabbard Visits Selma: "There Is More Work To Be Done." | TULSI 2020". 2019. TULSI2020.Com. Accessed October 11 2019. https://www.tulsi2020.com/press/2019-03-04-tulsi-gabbard-visits-selma-there-more-work-be-done.

campaign media is remarkable. Any video, of any length, can be shared completely for free. Though it does require some extra labor to cultivate a large enough following to ensure people see them, that's a trade-off well worth making. Don't be fooled: it doesn't take marrying a cinematographer to harness the power of social media videography. In fact, it is more than possible to use similar tactics without professional equipment and in lower-profile races.

While working on Thad Gray's campaign for Connecticut State Treasurer in 2018, I accompanied him to the Stony Hill Brewery in Branford one summer evening. Here, we attended an event called "Pints and Politics: Contractors & Candidates." Only a week before Connecticut's primary election, the brewery was filled to the brim with local contractors and candidates running for statewide offices. I followed Thad in, equipped with palm cards, stickers, and my trusty DSLR camera. As he circulated around the room, I snapped away from behind. Each time he started conversing with someone new, I had a mission: capture at least five photos and one video clip from each interaction, making a special effort to record handshakes and laughs. The next morning, I brought my camera and laptop over to Catherine Marx, Thad's campaign manager. We sat side-by-side at her kitchen table, perusing footage. As soon as we came across flattering photo or video, we flagged it. We drafted a brief message about the event, then sent it to Thad to record and send back in as a voice memo. I looked to YouTube's copyright-free music library to find a light, cheerful melody.

Within a few minutes, we had a complete video on our hands. The music chirps, clips and stills from the event begin to roll, and Thad narrates, "It was great to be at the Stony Brook Brewery in Branford talking to contractors who are small business owners. We know that it's time to take back Connecticut! Vote Thad Gray for State Treasurer." This video was not fancy. It took just one morning to make. It was only eighteen seconds long—kept short to avoid being boring per Catherine's advice. I used Windows Movie Maker, which come free on all PCs. This approach turned a routine campaign stop into a prime media opportunity. It let us show Thad engaging with a key, blue-collar constituency in a friendly environment. Not only was he able to impact those he spoke to directly, but also those who heard his voice and saw his face online. It quickly became one of the most popular videos on our Facebook page.

Once again, nothing too fancy required. The point is to showcase the candidate's whereabouts and positions in a way that builds a digital relationship between themselves and potential voters. A novice cameraman, some entry-level editing software, and a little creativity does the trick.

HOW SOCIAL MEDIA OPENS A NEW FRONTIER

Social media has undeniably shaken up the way national, statewide, and local campaigning functions. However, because it's a relatively new phenomenon not everyone in the political world is yet savvy. While large-scale campaigns now come equipped with comprehensive media teams, local ones may not have anyone onboard with digital acumen.In this moment, harnessing the power of technological innovation requires all parties to be willing.

HOW WE CAN ALL USE THIS TO OUR ADVANTAGE

Candidates need to understand and embrace technology, even if they've been around for decades and don't see the point. Things as simple as being in pictures, recording video messages, or directly posting updates allows for connection with more voters than ever possible before. Many within younger generations use social media daily, so ignoring this key demographic substantially decreases visibility.

Voters also need to actively seek out and engage with political postings. It's easier than ever to see, hear, and learn about local politics. When a boosted ad pops up, watch it and even click on the candidate's page. Follow candidates on Facebook and Instagram if they catch your attention. If you need to make up your mind before voting, pull up social media and watch their videos, see their pictures, and read their messages to decide for yourself what you think. There are even ways to send messages or leave comments, creating interactive engagement.Finally, volunteers and staffers are necessary to keep campaigns afloat. Though doable, taking pictures, editing videos, and crafting posts requires time and manpower. These tasks may be difficult for a baby boomer to take on but are generally very manageable for a millennial or Gen Z-er who grew up with it. With a wide variety of tasks during a campaign, social media is becoming increasingly critical. It's important that my generation knows these opportunities exist, ready to be taken on. One may expect campaign work to be repetitive and bland, but this new side of things is exciting, artistic, and challenging.

With these groups on board, we can progress into the modern marketplace of political media, where staying educated, engaged, and involved is easier than ever.

CHAPTER 10:

GOING LOCAL

—

As we approach the end, I'd like to take a moment to thank you for reading. While writing, I increasingly allowed more personal stories than planned. I couldn't help but share memories, experiences, and takeaways from my time as a spectator and tenure as a volunteer. On the local level, all of these real moments—even if small—are relevant.

This process began with interviews with established political figures in my area. Though the sample size may seem small—mostly people from Connecticut—that's what local politics is all about. I opted to highlight a few within my bubble, but there are so many more local figures out there.

Ron Deb isn't America's only college-aged campaign manager, and Jay Moran isn't the only across-the-aisle reaching mayor. There are people like Chris Healy strategically over-seeing campaigns with expert eyes, just as there are others like Art Linares, going out on a limb when everyone else seems older and more experienced. People like this exist across the country—even near you.

Everyone in local politics, Republican or Democrat, volunteer or paid official, Northerner or Southerner, is there because they want to be. The felt compelled in some way, and they acted on it.This book attempted to demystify that process, how it works, and how it can be replicated by those who haven't yet stepped forward.

WHY WE CAN ALL LEARN SOMETHING

We all have political perceptions. Some of us like it and some of us hate it. Some of us are invested in the local, while many more of us are more invested in the national. Regardless, many have misconceptions of what politics is truly about. It'll never be totally cleansed of corruption, polarization, and outrage—but we can distance ourselves from these by paying more attention to what's happening locally: where real people, in real communities, solve real issues.

I learned this after getting involved. I wanted to write about it to spread knowledge, broadcast the lessons I've learned, and honor the individuals I've learned from along the way.

I wanted to let people into my political circle. I wanted to acquaint people not with infamous faces in Washington, D.C., but regular people in regular places who support our nation's political system without true recognition.

Though I was hooked in by of media-covered partisan-driven national-scale politics (I still keep track, only slightly less religiously), once I met those on-the-ground my perspective changed.

HOW IT ENDS

I began writing this book as a college senior. 2019 is an off-year, the midterm elections are behind us, and the general election isn't until next year. Thinking there would be no immediate campaign-world opportunities post-graduation, writing this book could keep me involved with the subject I loved.I was wrong. After graduating, I returned home. My plan was to continue writing, apply to graduate school, and take on whatever else came my way. Soon after returning, however, I went to dinner with Lorraine Marchetti. As we reminisced about her old campaign, the conversation shifted from past to present. She asked what I'd be up to now; I let her know that I was open to anything. That evening, she invited me to an executive board meeting of the Glastonbury Republican Town Committee. Once there, I saw some familiar faces from years past, and got to listen while they deliberated. I let them know I was around and willing to help, and that was the end of it.

A few weeks later, I got a call from Lorraine about a potential opportunity. Later that day, I spoke with John Tanski, the GRTC's chairman. By evening, I was officially campaign manager for a slate of Glastonbury Republicans running for seats on the Town Council, Board of Education, and others.

It's one thing to speak abstractly about the benefits of local political involvement—it's another to actually live through them. Last night, I was in a meeting with my campaign team. Each week, I make up an agenda, we sit around a table, and discuss what we have to do next. Every morning and every evening, we stand on a different corner with our signs and wave to those who drive by while strengthening our relationships with one another. The team is newcomers and old hands alike, all excited about campaigning and laser-focused on the issues facing our community. We lead separate lives but come together as friends and teammates. When we brainstormed ideas for a bumper sticker design, one suggestion stood out: "Keep it Local."

ACKNOWLEDGEMENTS

As senior year of college was approaching, I noticed many of my peers committing to writing theses. While I admired the value of such an undertaking and had the time and commitment to put into one, no academic topic spoke to me quite enough. Fortunately, at the same time, Katie Rogers (my friend from high school) introduced me to Professor Eric Koester, who introduced a different kind of capstone to consider.

Though I didn't initially plan for this to be the case, *Big Little Politics* ultimately became my professional coming-of-age story. Not only does it highlight lessons I've learned and moments I've experienced over my four years of local political involvement but also details from my formative, childhood years to add some context for how I got there. It was not easy to cohesively and logically put all of this together, but with the help of my editors Cortni Merritt and Kristy Carter, fragmented thoughts and memories became refined stories and chapters. However, the only reason any of this was possible is because I wrote about a topic that I am passionate about. This enthusiasm was cultivated by those I had the privilege of working with, who introduced me to this world and encouraged me to keep going. I'd like to thank Chris Healy, who I could truly listen to for hours, Catherine Marx, who activated my potential and cheered me on along the way, and Judy Stearns, who represents local political involvement at its finest.

I'd also like to extend a special thank you to Lorraine Marchetti, whose name popped up many times over the course of the book. A former boss, a current mentor, and a permanent friend, she has been beside me since day one and continues to introduce me to more than I could have ever imagined. I would not be on this path today if it weren't for her.

Big Little Politics also includes interviews I conducted with other figures near to me, whose stories fit perfectly into the book's message, so thank you to Ron Deb, Art Linares, and Jay Moran for giving me the time for a personal interview.

I'd also like to thank my friends for putting up with my irregular work schedule and trips home to campaign. I'd like to thank my family as well for ghostwriting postcards, looking over my videos before posting, and supporting my pursuits in this less-than-lucrative industry.

Finally, I'd like to acknowledge that final leg of my authorial journey coincided with another endeavor: managing a campaign. Over late 2019, I ran a municipal campaign for team that included six Town Council candidates and three Board of Education candidates, which put me face to face with all aspects of local politics. I'd first like to thank these candidates for entrusting me with such a wide scope of responsibilities that allowed me to sharpen my own skills significantly. More importantly, I'd like to thank every one of them for dedicating so much time and energy to supporting our community and demonstrating firsthand the importance of accessible, local leadership. Keep it Local!

APPENDIX

———

INTRODUCTION

"Connecticut State Senate District 4 – Ballotpedia". 2019. Ballotpedia. Accessed October 11 2019. https://ballotpedia.org/Connecticut_State_Senate_District_4.

Desjardins, Lisa, and Daniel Bush. 2016. „The Trump Campaign Has A Ground-Game Problem". *PBS Newshour.* Accessed October 11 2019. https://www.pbs.org/newshour/politics/trump-campaign-has-ground-game-problem.

CHAPTER 1

"2020 Hopeful Pete Buttigieg Touts "More Experience In Government" Than Trump". 2019. Cbsnews.Com. Accessed

October 11 2019. https://www.cbsnews.com/news/indiana-mayor-pete-buttigieg-touts-more-experience-in-government-than-trump/.

Baptiste, Nathalie. 2019. "Why South Bend's Police Department Has Become A Campaign Issue For Mayor Pete". Mother Jones. Accessed October 11 2019. https://www.motherjones.com/politics/2019/07/why-south-bends-police-department-has-become-a-campaign-issue-for-mayor-pete/.

Buttigieg, Pete. 2017. "Hitting Home: A New Politics Of The Everyday". Medium. Accessed October 11 2019. https://medium.com/the-moment-by-pete-for-america/hitting-home-a-new-politics-of-the-everyday-76316121f06a.

"How Does South Bend Feel About 'Mayor Pete' For President?". 2019. Youtube. Accessed October 11 2019. https://www.youtube.com/watch?v=cgMuPErHxZY&t=81s.

McCarthy, Tom, and Martin Pengelly. 2019. "'They Call Me Mayor Pete': Buttigieg Launches 2020 Presidential Run". The Guardian. Accessed October 11 2019. https://www.theguardian.com/us-news/2019/apr/14/pete-buttigieg-2020-presidential-campaign-launch.

"Pete Buttigieg, "Shortest Way Home"". 2019. Youtube. Accessed October 11 2019. https://www.youtube.com/watch?v=Nldx3r7h3Cg.

"Presidential Hopeful Pete Buttigieg Talks 2020, New Memoir | Season 2019 Episode 02/13/2019 | Chicago Tonight". 2019. PBS.Org. Accessed October 11 2019. https://www.pbs.org/video/presidential-hopeful-pete-buttigieg-talks-2020-new-memoir-ky/.

CHAPTER 2

Graydon, Shari. 2010. "Commentary Vs Reporting". Informedopinions.Org. Accessed October 11 2019. https://informedopinions.org/commentary-vs-reporting/

Mitchell, Amy, Jeffery Gottfried, Jocelyn Kiley, and Katerina Eva Matsa. 2014. "Political Polarization & Media Habits". Pew Research Center's Journalism Project. Accessed October 11 2019. https://www.journalism.org/2014/10/21/political-polarization-media-habits/.

CHAPTER 3

Dumcius, Gintautas. 2016. "Poll: Only 46 Percent Of Americans Know Each State Has Two U.S. Senators". Masslive.

Accessed October 11 2019. https://www.masslive.com/
politics/2016/03/edward_m_kennedy_institute_pol.html.

Freiling, Nick. 2017. "Just 37% Of Americans Can Name
Their Representative | Haven Insights". Haven Insights.
Accessed October 11 2019. https://www.haveninsights.
com/just-37-percent-name-representative/.

Hajnal, Zoltan. 2018. "Opinion | Why Does No One Vote
In Local Elections?". Nytimes.Com. Accessed October 11
2019. https://www.nytimes.com/2018/10/22/opinion/why-
does-no-one-vote-in-local-elections.html.

Plumer, Brad. 2016. "Why 100 Million Americans Won't
Vote On Tuesday". Vox. Accessed October 11 2019. https://
www.vox.com/policy-and-politics/2016/11/7/13536198/elec-
tion-day-americans-vote.

CHAPTER 5

"Glastonbury RTC Chair John Tanski Nominates Rep. Prasad
Srinivasan For Governor". 2019. Youtube. Accessed Octo-
ber 11 2019. https://www.youtube.com/watch?v=s76oHS-
NIxtk.

CHAPTER 7

Edwards-Levy, Ariel. 2016. "Volunteering For A Campaign Or Going To Rallies? You're In The Minority." Huffington Post. Accessed October 11 2019. https://www.huffpost.com/entry/campaign-volunteering-rallies-poll_n_581906b8e4b0f96eba968ca7?guccounter=1&guce_referrer=aHR0cHM6Ly93d3cuZ29vZ2xlLmNvbvbS8&guce_referrer_sig=AQAAAKZ5jU9aXPg8RL-JufkquM6FHkUb6gb-hWI34DKaTTTpR-tqObD-plgBKQLZq3jAfF2GOO_C4Ksjk4KePhLIj6L5LuN-FHqydRMQn3OFmOc1T-Y-q74iurBrpLUf5XETH-ByeAlAfD-m5tKbmv5YxdHHi-zwwRVYNoKcwRD8J-MiKqb_M

CHAPTER 8

"Episode 18: Amanda Litman '12 On Her Passion For Progressive Politics". 2019. Alumni.Northwestern.Edu. Accessed October 11 2019. https://www.alumni.northwestern.edu/s/1479/02-naa/16/interior.aspx?pgid=28858&gid=2&cid=50056.

Kurts, Karl. 2015. "Who We Elect: The Demographics Of State Legislatures ". 2015. Ncsl.Org. Accessed October 11 2019. http://www.ncsl.org/research/about-state-legislatures/who-we-elect.aspx.

"Our 2019–2020 Strategic Plan". 2019. Medium. Accessed October 11 2019. https://medium.com/@runforsomething/run-for-somethings-2019-2020-strategic-plan-a272e5633849.

CHAPTER 9

Erickson, David. 2017. "US Political Ad Spend Allocations – 2016 Vs 2012 [CHART] – E-Strategy Trends". E-Strategy Marketing Trends. Accessed October 11 2019. http://trends.e-strategyblog.com/2017/06/14/us-political-ad-spending-allocations-2012-vs-2016/28442?fbclid=IwARorjgKE86q7kEjBx9EMpkfBxENHDolD-Su7y6RjAEOgaNIpngvA9kjKRFbA.

Joyella, Mark. 2016. "10 Iconic Presidential Campaign Ads That Changed Political Advertising". Adweek.Com. Accessed October 11 2019. https://www.adweek.com/tv-video/10-iconic-presidential-campaign-ads-changed-political-advertising-172600/.

Kapko, Matt. 2016. "How Social Media Is Shaping The 2016 Presidential Election". CIO. Accessed October 11 2019. https://www.cio.com/article/3125120/how-social-media-is-shaping-the-2016-presidential-election.html.

"Tulsi Gabbard Visits Selma: "There Is More Work To Be Done." | TULSI 2020". 2019. TULSI2020.Com. Accessed October 11 2019. https://www.tulsi2020.com/press/2019-03-04-tulsi-gabbard-visits-selma-there-more-work-be-done.

"Tulsi TV – On The Road – Episode 3: Laconia, Plymouth". 2019. Youtube. Accessed October 11 2019. https://www.youtube.com/watch?v=iwjclSoI9UU.

* 9 7 8 1 6 4 1 3 7 3 0 3 6 *